a
christian
approach
to
sexuality

john w. miller

Mennonite Publishing House,
Scottdale, Pennsylvania

*"Have you not read
that the creator from the beginning
made them male and female
and that he said:
'This is why a man must leave father and mother,
and cling to his wife,
and the two become one body'?
They are no longer two, therefore,
but one body.
So then,
what God has united,
man must not divide."* *
JESUS*

*Matthew 19:4-6.

contents

preface

It never occurred to me that I would ever write a book on sex. That I have done so is partly the result of a seminar for ministers which met during the winter of 1970-71 and for which I was responsible. In the course of this seminar the question of a Christian approach to divorce and remarriage was raised, and rather relentlessly pursued for an eight-month period. We naturally went to the Scriptures for guidance, and to the teachings of Jesus in particular. In the process of doing so, I was compelled to realize how uncertain was our reading of His much-debated words on this subject, and how partial our grasp of what is really taking place in the revolution in sexual thinking now in progress in the modern world. A double search began for a deeper understanding of Jesus' sexual teachings, on the one hand, and for more clarity, on the other, as to the presuppositions of modern sexual thinking.

Since that time I have not been able to terminate this search. The following manuscript should be thought of as only a first draft, so to speak, of some preliminary discoveries. I would not, of course, be audacious enough to submit it for publication did I not believe that I have come to some possibly helpful answers to certain facets of this subject area.

In particular I am grateful for the realization, very slow and hard in coming, that Jesus' teachings on divorce and remarriage are more in the nature of "wisdom sayings" than laws. They provide "insight" into reality in the tradition of Jewish wise men, more than they legislate in the tradition of Old Testament codes. As such they evoke a vivid impression of Jesus' love of life over against all that would lead us away from our highest God-given potential. This realization has significantly enlarged my sense of the relevance of Jesus' thought for contemporary sexual thinking and may be one of the more substantial contributions of the following study.

I am acutely aware, however, that precisely in the application of Jesus' teachings to modern trends, I have perhaps dealt all too inadequately with many of the topics chosen for discussion. While it was the specific issue of divorce and remarriage that prompted this study, it soon became clear that this one issue could be rightly dealt with only in the context of the total process of sexual rethinking now in progress.

As I was writing and working on this subject, I also became increasingly aware of the confusion that prevails among Christians, no less than others, about sexual ideals generally. Rightly has one prominent journalist, Vance Packard, characterized our times as a "sexual wilderness." It is for this reason that I have extended the discussion to include not only a fairly wide range of sexual problems, but some comments relevant to sexual healing as well. Especially in this latter category the following study does little more than scratch the surface, but I did at least want to do that, in order to indicate the direction that the approach suggested might take in this important enterprise.

In preparing the final version of this manuscript, I had in mind the possibility that it might be useful for group study. On this account I tried to write simply, although at times the material itself defied my powers to do so. For the same reason I have added a few study suggestions which are found in the appendix.

Even with a booklet as modest as this one, a word of thanks is due to many. In this case, however, it must be said with special emphasis that such acknowledgements in no way implicate the persons involved in the final product. Different approaches still abound to the problems dealt with in the following pages, and some of those who have helped me most will no doubt remain uneasy with what I have written.

Nevertheless, I would feel delinquent did I not mention their names and record the gratitude I feel. Ross Bender, currently of the Mennonite Board of Congregational Ministries, twice read the manuscript in various stages of preparation, and each time wrote an extensive critical review that proved stimulating and helpful. I have also benefited from the critical comments of Robert Showalter, a Virginia psychiatrist; Ella May Miller, of the *Heart to Heart* radio program; John Howard Yoder, of the Goshen Biblical Seminary; Albert Meyer of Goshen College; Peter Letkemann and J. Howard Kauffman, Mennonite sociologists; and Father Don Dietrick, of the St. Aloysius Parish (Kitchener).

Special mention is also due the Mennonite ministers of Ontario who shared with me in the beginning stages of the search that prompted this study, as well as several house church groups and an adult Sunday school class at the Erb Street Mennonite Church in Waterloo, Ontario, where the chapters of this booklet were given their first trial run as a study resource. My thanks too to Levi Miller, editor at Mennonite Publishing House, whose interest in this manuscript was decisive in its being published at this time.

It goes without saying that my wife played a very special role in the development of this essay. My children too deserve credit for their good humor and understanding while their father pored, days on end, over a desk piled with sex literature.

Let me conclude this preface by confessing to a certain ambivalence toward moving forward with a project of this kind. The trends of our time compel us to think, talk, and write about human sexuality as never before in human history. But the reserve of an earlier generation toward this subject was not without reason. Human sexuality is a "great mystery," the Apostle Paul once wisely said. In the end it defies our powers of rational analysis. "The flash of it is a flash of fire," wrote the poet in the Song of Songs, "a flame of Yahweh himself" (8:6). It will be a better day when books about human sexuality such as this one can be put aside in renewed awareness of the mystery itself.

John W. Miller
February, 1973

introduction

A debate is now in progress in the modern world, the outcome of which may well affect lives as profoundly as any other single event. Under question are the norms that shall counsel persons in fashioning a sexual life worthy to be called human.

As the debate proceeds more and more voices are being heard, among them the medical specialist, the anthropologist, the psychiatrist, the sociologist, the historian, and the theologian. And out of this rising chorus of "experts" a consensus is beginning to emerge. Many of the sexual standards of the past are being abandoned in favor of greater sexual freedom. Sexual intercourse among the unmarried as well as extramarital affairs no longer carry the stigma they once did. While the right to divorce and remarry is made easier, a growing number of couples dispense with marriage rites altogether and live "common law." Sexual practices once thought of as deviant, such as masturbation, homosexuality, and pornography are increasingly tolerated, if not outrightly approved.

The magnitude of these changes can hardly be grasped even by those living in the midst of them. "Sexual mores in the United States," wrote Vance Packard, in 1971, "have changed more dramatically in the past five years than in the preceding forty years. And openness in exposure of the human body — has become more commonplace in the Western world than at any time in the past 1,600 years." [1]

Another author identifies 1969 as the "turning point" in this avalanche of sexual permissiveness, the year "when there was really no turning back." [2] He cites the following items as evidence: the miniskirt, uni-sex clothing, Hugh Hefner, the pill, popular demand for abortion law repeal, masturbatory dances, rock lyrics, growing scorn of virginity, *Myra Breckenridge*, rise in the divorce rate, and the Beatles.

Among the young this new permissiveness has been characterized as "a 'hang-loose' ethic that involves irreverence for traditional standards, a broad tolerance of the behavior of others, strong emphasis upon humanism, a courting of raw experience, and an intense focusing upon NOW." [3] "What we are observing all about us then," writes Philip Zimbardo of Stanford University, "is a sudden change in the restraints that normally control the expression of our drives, impulses, emotions." [4]

The possible effect of this "sudden change" in sexual restraints on the venerable institution of marriage is forecast in recent statistics from Sweden, a society that stands in the forefront of the sexual revolution. A 1972 report from the Swedish state statistical bureau shows a 35 percent decline in marriages between 1966 and 1971, the result apparently of the increase in informal sexual relations. In the same period illegitimacy rose to 18 percent of all births, a 10 percent rise from 1960.

Alvin Toffler, in his widely acclaimed book, *Future Shock*, predicts that serial monogamy (one marriage after another) will soon replace permanent monogamy ("till death do us part") as the major form of modern marriage.

How shall Christians respond to this avalanche of sexual change? It is common knowledge that not only society at large is locked in debate of these changing norms. A debate rages within the Christian church itself, with leading Christian spokesmen taking contradictory positions on almost every item of the discussion. A case in point is the widely circulated book, *Honest Sex* (1968), by Rustum and Della Roy. Taking the point of view of those theologians who advocate a flexible rather than a legalistic approach to sexual conduct, the Roys conclude their exploration of sexual options for Christians by portraying a norm that includes guilt-free masturbation, petting to orgasm, and sexual intercourse before marriage, as well as polygamous relations afterward.

In the face of such novel and often contradictory values on the part of Christians themselves, how can one hope to fashion an approach to human sexuality that goes by that name?

This question, I suggest, inevitably raises another: Are there

8

higher authorities in the Christian church to which one can turn for guidance in matters of this kind? Is there anywhere a wisdom so unimpeachable that one can refer to it as the foundation on which to build a sexual point of view?

Traditionally the church has answered this query with a resounding "yes!" In recent years, however, this "yes" has been somewhat muted because of a growing number of difficulties associated with two of the church's better known answers to the authority question. Because these difficulties have contributed significantly to the confusion now rampant in the Christian church, not only in the face of the modern sexual revolution, but in other matters as well, they must be considered briefly.

Until recently the two most widely respected authorities among Christians were the pope in Roman Catholicism, and the Bible among Protestants. In both cases these authorities came to be thought of as infallible and hence completely reliable without fear of error.

It is well known, however, how in recent days the Roman Catholic dogma of papal infallibility has suffered erosion, especially in the wake of Pope Paul's teaching on birth control.

Protestants for their part, already at the time of the sixteenth-century Reformation, had rejected this dogma and put in its place the doctrine of an infallible Bible. But this approach too has fallen on hard times. Growing familiarity with the totality of biblical literature has demonstrated both the unity and the considerable diversity of its doctrinal content. It has become increasingly clear to many that when the pages of the Bible are consulted by the church for authoritative teaching, a *selective* approach is invariably followed. But that raises the question: selective on what basis? If we turn to the Bible for guidance, to which parts do we turn, and why to those parts and not to others? Questions of this kind have been raised but not always adequately answered, with the consequence that the Bible, like the pope, functions among us less authoritatively than it once did.

In the wake of this failure of the two older answers to the authority question, a third one is beginning to emerge in the Christian churches, one that I believe may help us with the task to which we are addressing ourselves in this study. In this third approach neither pope nor Bible *as a whole* are vested with final authority. Instead we are invited to turn to that One who is everywhere recognized as the Founder and Lord of the church, Jesus of Nazareth. His words and deeds recorded in the pages of the New Testament and available for study in those documents called the Gospels are given primacy as the foundation on which the church builds its faith and life.

This answer corresponds better than the ones referred to above to Jesus' own point of view. The Gospels make it abundantly clear how He called disciples and bound them to Himself and His own teachings as the way to salvation. Luke 9:26. It is also well known how after the resurrection the early Christians gathered His words into collections that became the basis of instruction for all new members of their community. In doing this they gave to Jesus and His teachings first place of authority in their ranks. [5]

To the question then, "Where can we turn as Christians for guidance in the sexual wilderness?" the answer will be: *To the Founder of Christianity, Jesus of Nazareth, and to the weighty words He spoke on this subject.*

Making this suggestion is not meant to depreciate the help that can be found elsewhere in ancient or modern times. Above all, there is no desire to indicate any lack of respect for other parts of the Bible. In this study of Jesus' thoughts on human sexuality it shall quickly be seen how He linked His teachings on this subject to several focal Scriptures from the Old Testament. This in itself is evidence as to how much He valued those writings and saw His ideas in continuity with them.

Also in the New Testament canon outside of the Gospels there are texts that should and will nourish the Christian consciousness about human sexuality and marriage as long as the church exists. Here too it can be shown how much these texts in turn rely upon older traditions, including now the insights of Jesus Himself.

The point then is not that one should confine a study of this or any other area of human existence to the few words spoken by Jesus, but that *we should begin with them,* as the early church itself did, *and give them a prior and decisive place in our thinking.*

When we do so, we shall make an important discovery. The authority of Jesus is no arbitrary act, but truth itself intuitively perceived. In the case of human sexuality, as shall be seen, Jesus only taught what He maintained was there for anyone to see, for this side of life belongs to the order of God willed from creation. That is why Christian sexual morality in the final analysis, while taking its clues from Jesus, is no blind obedience to His or any other laws on the subject, but rather a wisdom that manifests itself wherever men and women do not harden their hearts to what they are.

In summary: the widespread questioning of sexual ideals in the world at large was noted as well as the debate that is now in progress in the Christian church itself. In searching how to respond to this highly confusing situation, the question of authority in the church was briefly explored. Can anyone help us find the way?

Traditionally the church has answered this question by pointing to pope or Bible, but this has led to certain difficulties. The pope, it would seem, is capable of mistakes even in his most soberly formulated teachings, and the Bible as a whole, while united by certain fundamental themes, is at the same time full of diversities, demanding a selective approach. The alternative purposed here is to begin this exploration by looking at the insights of Jesus, the universally recognized Founder and Leader of the Christian church. There is a wisdom there, that has commended itself to men of good will.

---

1. Vance Packard, in a symposium entitled *Sexual Latitude, for and against,* 1971, p. 85.
2. John Hudson, *Ibid.*, p. 165.
3. *Vance Packard,* Ibid., p. 86.
4. Quoted by Vance Packard, *Ibid.*, p. 87.
5. On the use of Jesus' teachings as early Christian catechism, see J. Jeremias, *The Sermon on the Mount,* 1963, and J. Miller, *The Christian Way,* 1969.

study suggestions

If this book is used in a group context, study suggestions can be found in the Appendix beginning on page 105.

1. jesus' teaching about divorce and remarriage

This chapter and the one to follow will look at Jesus' sexual teachings against the background of the world in which they were first given. Only when His words are understood as they were intended to be understood in first-century Palestine can we begin to apply them to the world today.

The fund of Jesus' sexual teachings is small. The same might be said of His teachings as a whole. An early Christian apologist, Justin Martyr, took note of this fact when he wrote: "His sayings were short and concise, for He was no sophist, but His Word was the power of God."

In sexual matters Jesus' teachings focus primarily on one issue: the question of marriage and its permanence. Even with reference to this one topic there are just two groups of sayings, one of them criticizing the practice of divorce and remarriage, and the other giving reasons for this surprising criticism.

This chapter will focus on Jesus' words in criticism of divorce and remarriage. Chapter two will look at His defense of His critique.

I.

Before examining Jesus' teaching against divorce and remarriage, one might ask why Jesus confined Himself so exclusively to this one problem in sexual life. The answer lies in an understanding of the world in which He lived.

The crucial point is this: the Jewish community of first-century Palestine had a firm set of sexual standards at almost every point, except for divorce and remarriage. Premarital sexual intercourse, for example, was strictly prohibited. Homosexuality was looked upon as a perversion. Sexual relations between a man and another man's wife were forbidden by the seventh commandment against adultery. Monogamy had established itself firmly as the highest ideal of marriage. *On only one question was the Jewish community divided: What reasons justify divorce and remarriage?*

Even here, it should be pointed out the question was not *whether* divorce and remarriage are permissible. On that issue too the Jewish community was united. A man may put away his wife, under certain circumstances, and marry another. But under *what* circumstances? On that one question only there existed an unresolved debate.

Since the Jewish leaders of the first century viewed the laws of the Old Testament as divine revelation, they sought an answer to this question by studying those laws. One law in particular came under consideration: Deuteronomy 24:1 ff. In order to understand Jesus' teaching, one needs to look briefly at this Scripture, as well as at the way in which the Jewish community interpreted it.

II.

"Supposing a man has taken a wife and consummated the marriage; but she has not pleased him and he has found some impropriety of which to accuse her; so he has made out a writ of divorce for her and handed it to her and then dismissed her from his house; she leaves his home and goes away to become the wife of another man. If this other man takes a dislike to her and makes out a writ of divorce for her and hands it to her and dismisses her from his house (or if this other man who took her as his wife happens to die), her first husband, who has repudiated her, may not take her back as his wife now that she has been defiled in this way. For that is detestable in the sight of Yahweh, and you must not bring guilt on the land that Yahweh your God gives for your inheritance." (Deut. 24:1-4).

It should be observed, first of all, that the law in Deuteronomy 24:1-4 does *not* speak directly to the question of divorce and remarriage. Rather it lays down the principle that when divorce has *already* taken place, the divorced wife may not return to her first husband, should she remarry and then lose her second husband. The Jewish law considers her to be "defiled" (24:4) by the second marriage, and her return to the original husband, under these circumstances, is called "detestable."

If then Deuteronomy 24:1-4 does not address itself specifically to the question of divorce and remarriage, it obviously does *assume* that divorce and remarriage may take place under certain circumstances, and it hints at what the justifying reasons might be. But what are they? Here is where the argument focused.

The clauses under debate were these: ". . . but she has not pleased him and he has found *some impropriety* of which to accuse her. . . ." What is meant by the two words "some impropriety"? This was the crux of the debate.

There were two schools of thought. One school, led by the conservative Rabbi Shammai, interpreted these words as referring exclusively to *sexual* misconduct. The other school, under the leadership of the more liberal Rabbi Hillel, artificially separated the words "some" and "impropriety" and argued that there are *two* reasons for divorce given here: "some" and "impropriety"! In other words almost anything could qualify as the reason for divorce. This latter school also noted that the text says: ". . . but she has not pleased him. . . ." Whatever then would cause a wife to fall out of favor with her husband, whether burning his meal or another more beautiful woman, could justifiably lead to divorce and remarriage.

It is not difficult to believe the historians Philo and Josephus when they tell us that this lax approach toward divorce and remarriage was the one that prevailed among the Jews of Palestine in the time of Jesus. Divorce and remarriage were rampant in certain classes and made all the more so by the ease with which the husband could dismiss his wife. All that was needed was to write out a bill of particulars and make sure that she received it. On the other hand, custom dictated that only the husband could act in such a cavalier fashion. For the wife, the right to initiate divorce against her husband was nonexistent, or virtually so.

This then was the background against which Jesus gave His own special teachings on marriage — a background characterized by extraordinary strictness in the area of premarital and extramarital sex, but equally extraordinary permissiveness when it came to divorce and remarriage.

That Jesus shared the convictions of His Jewish contemporaries regarding premarital and extramarital sex cannot be doubted. His strong words against both adulterous acts and thoughts are well known. Matthew 5:27 f. He left no similar words on the question of premarital sex (unless it would be the reference to "fornication" in Matthew 15:19). But as shall be seen, sex before marriage is excluded by Jesus' very definition of marriage. In their negative attitude toward premarital and extramarital sex Jesus and His contemporaries were firmly united.

The same cannot be said, however, for the debated issue of divorce and remarriage. To this question, records would indicate, Jesus spoke with an emphasis that surprised both His disciples and His opponents. What did He say?

III.

At this point one must carefully examine the first of the two groups of sayings referred to above: *the one in criticism of divorce and remarriage.* No less than five times in the New Testament a brief teaching by Jesus on this subject is encountered, four times in the Gospels (Matthew 5:32; 19:9; Mark 10: 11 f.; Luke 16:18) and once in Paul's Corinthian letter (1 Corinthians 7:10 f.). Although the form of the saying in each instance varies slightly, it would appear that we have a single saying which was translated and adapted in a variety of ways to meet the needs of the Christian church in its very diverse localities.

In order to see at a glance the similarities and diversities in the saying under discussion, all five versions are listed in a single column:

Luke 16:18

"Every one who divorces his wife and marries another commits adultery, and he who marries a woman divorced from her husband commits adultery."

Mark 10:11 f.

"Whoever divorces his wife and marries another, commits adultery against her; and if she divorces her husband and marries another, she commits adultery."

15

1 Corinthians 7:10

The wife should not separate
from her husband (but if she
does, let her remain single or
else be reconciled to her
husband) —

and the husband should
not divorce his wife.

Matthew 5:32

"Every one who divorces his wife,
except on the ground of
unchastity, makes her an
adulteress;

and whoever marries
a divorced woman
commits adultery."

Matthew 19:9

Whoever divorces his wife,
except for unchastity,
and marries another,
commits adultery.

(RSV translation)

Without going into a detailed analysis of the variations that
appear, the following comments may prove helpful in sorting out
the major problems connected with the interpretation of this
text:

1. Some variations can be explained by considering how the
teachings of Jesus were transmitted in the early church. It is
well known that Jesus Himself did not write His teachings down.
No rabbi of His time did that. Teaching was by oral instruction
to a group of students or disciples.

The teachings of Jesus then were received and transmitted
orally by Jesus' first disciples to those who came to believe in
Him as Lord and Savior. As Christianity spread into the
Graeco-Roman world, these teachings were translated from Aramaic (Jesus' mother tongue) to Greek. In this way Jesus' words
became the regulating insights for the building up of the first
Christian churches. In other words, they were preserved, not
as museum pieces, but as living instruction for a growing reli-

gious movement. In this process the sayings were adapted to serve the needs of the various churches in different parts of the world.

The outstanding example of this is Paul's free quotation of Jesus' "command" (as he calls it) concerning divorce and remarriage. 1 Corinthians 7:10. Obviously Paul is not quoting this command verbatim, but in substance. The saying is a living idea for him, which he does not hesitate to introduce as a firm guideline for the complicated marital problems his converts in Corinth are facing.

2. But it was not only Paul who adapted this saying to meet the needs of his churches. This diverse use of the teaching in the early Christian churches is also reflected in the variations that appear in the Gospels as well. For example, the version of the saying in Luke 16:18 focuses only on *the husband's* action in divorce and remarriage. The same is true in the two texts in Matthew's Gospel. In Mark 10:11 f., however (as in 1 Corinthians 7:10 f.), divorce and remarriage on the part of both husband *and wife* are brought under review. A possible explanation for this variation comes to mind when one remembers the setting in which Jesus originally gave His teaching. Among Jesus' Jewish contemporaries in Palestine, as was noted, the problem of a wife divorcing her husband was nonexistent simply because a custom dictated against it. It is likely then that originally Jesus' saying focused only on the question of the husband's conduct. However, as the Christian mission moved out into the Graeco-Roman world, where wives also had the right to divorce, the church needed to revise the original saying slightly, so that it would apply (as it obviously should) to women as well.

3. The variation in this group of sayings, however, which stands out above the others and has given rise to a long and still continuing debate is *the so-called "exception clause" appearing only in Matthew 5:32 and Matthew 19:9.* Many biblical scholars have thought that this clause significantly modifies the sharp prohibition against divorce and remarriage laid down in the other versions of this saying. Whereas the saying as it appears in Mark and Luke (as well as in 1 Corinthians) prohibits divorce and remarriage *for any reason*, so these scholars argue, the Matthew texts allow for one exception, "except for unchastity." The usual interpretation is that this important

variation is a concession reflecting a declining marital standard in that part of the church represented by Matthew's Gospel. Jesus, it is said, forbade divorce and remarriage for any and every reason. But in the course of time the Matthean church permitted one exception to this strict rule: "except for unchastity." More recent study of these exception clauses, however, has raised a question about this line of interpretation.

For example, it is not quite true to say that the exception clause in Matthew 5:32 allows for divorce and remarriage. *This verse does not in fact speak of divorce and remarriage in so many words, but rather of the husband's responsibility in causing his wife to become an adulteress.* The husband who divorces his wife, *"makes her an adulteress . . .* except on the ground of unchastity." In other words, the husband who divorces his wife, puts her in the position where she will be vulnerable to forming a second sexual union. In this way he contributes to her adultery, *unless* of course *the wife herself* had already taken the initiative in breaking the marital bond ("except for unchastity").

It is a mistake then to read Matthew 5:32 as though it were saying anything significantly different from the versions of the saying without the exception clause. In both cases divorce and remarriage are viewed, without exception as adulterous.

It would also appear that Matthew 19:9 has no other point in view than this one. The issue is not whether in fact divorce and remarriage are adulterous. That, as shall be seen in chapter two, is the inevitable conclusion growing out of Jesus' understanding of marriage. Even in Matthew 19:9 the only issue is moral responsibility. If the man divorces his wife, he bears responsibility for the tragic consequences, unless of course the divorce took place in the wake of the wife's prior infidelity. Then indeed the husband may separate from his wife, but that is all. For him too, even under these circumstances, a second sexual union would be adulterous. [2]

In all five versions of this saying then Jesus is quoted as saying essentially the same thing, although phrasing and focus differ slightly from version to version. "Everyone who divorces his wife and marries another commits adultery (or makes her an adulteress, Matthew 5:32), and whoever marries a divorced woman commits adultery." [3]

IV.

A full interpretation of these words must await chapter two where an examination is made of Jesus' own comments in support of them. But a few further thoughts are in order at this point on the form of the saying, for *the precise meaning of this particular sentence is in part tied to its form.*

Significant first of all, is the fact that the saying begins with a "whoever" clause. "Whoever divorces his wife. . . ." If one turns to the law codes of the Old Testament, one finds many examples of laws that begin this way (for example, Exodus 21:15-17: "Whoever strikes his father or his mother. . . . Whoever steals a man. . . . Whoever curses his father or his mother . . ." RSV). Laws so formulated usually deal with matters of special importance to the community. For this reason they often conclude by specifying death as the penalty for their violation. For example: "Whoever sacrifices to any god, save to the Lord only, shall be utterly destroyed" (Ex. 22:20, RSV).

When therefore Jesus begins: "Whoever divorces his wife and marries another . . ." the people of his time would know that He is talking about an issue of great significance.

However, and this is now of crucial importance, *unlike* the Old Testament laws that begin this way, *Jesus does not conclude His saying with a penalty* (". . . he shall be utterly destroyed.") but an explanation (". . . he commits adultery.") This saying is a *declaration*, not an *imperative*; an *insight*, not a *command. In this saying Jesus is not so much legislating against divorce and remarriage as telling us what in fact happens when people do divorce and remarry. They commit adultery! Regardless of whether a bill of divorce is obtained and the new marriage is legally formalized, the second marriage is adulterous, no less than if these legal transactions were dispensed with.*

This saying begins to suggest that Jesus viewed marriage from a nonlegal point of view. Marriages are neither made nor terminated by documents, and those who think that they are, are only fooling themselves.

In this trenchant word Jesus begins to expose the superficial thinking about human sexuality, rampant in His day and today. His further thoughts on this subject will be taken up in the next chapter.

1. David Dungan, *The Teachings of Jesus in the Churches of Paul*, Fortress Press, 1971.
2. "All Jesus allows is the obvious (from the point of view of Jewish law) right that a husband not be required to live with an unfaithful wife, but may send her away. She through her own lust has broken with the Law of Creation. In this sense, Jesus does make an exception to the general rejection of divorce. But there is no compelling indication that the husband is then free to contract another marriage." David Dungan, *Ibid*, p. 114.
3. For an exceptionally thorough and balanced treatment of these texts see especially the book by David Dungan, *Ibid*. Additional brief but authoritative studies of these passages may be found in J. Jeremias, *N. T. Theology*, Vol. I , *The Proclamation of Jesus*, 1971, pp. 223 ff.; F. Beare, *The Earliest Records of Jesus*, 1962, pp. 181, 190 ff.; T. W. Manson, *The Sayings of Jesus*, 1963, pp. 200,

2. jesus' teaching in support of monogamy

According to parallel accounts in Matthew 19:1-9 and Mark 10:1-9, Jesus first made the sharp criticism of divorce and re-marriage, discussed in the previous chapter, on the occasion of a debate with "some Pharisees" who "approached him. . .to test him " (Mt. 19:3). Again there are minor variations between the parallel versions of this debate. Mark's report was apparently modified slightly to make it more relevant to the Gentile audience for which he was writing. Matthew's version records the encounter as it would have taken place in its Jewish setting. [1] Although there are no substantial differences between the two versions, where they do differ, we will follow the more original report as it appears in Matthew:

"Some Pharisees approached him, and to test him they said, 'Is it against the Law for a man to divorce his wife on any pretext whatever?' He answered, 'Have you not read that the creator from the beginning made them male and female and that he said: This is why a man must leave father and mother, and cling to his wife, and the two become one body? They are no longer two, therefore, but one body. So then, what God has united, man must not divide."

"They said to him, 'Then why did Moses command that a writ of dismissal should be given in cases of divorce?' 'It was because you were so unteachable,' he said, 'that Moses allowed you to divorce your wives, but it was not like this from the beginning. Now I say this to you: the man who divorces his wife — I am not speaking of fornication — and marries another, is guilty of adultery.' "

This brief passage is of paramount importance for understanding Jesus' approach to marriage in particular and human sexuality in general. Here one learns of the reasoning behind His shocking statement that divorce and remarriage are equivalent to adultery. Here He states His case for lifelong monogamy, a point of view that has been distinctive of Christianity since its earliest days.

The background is again the one noted in the previous chapter: the Jewish dispute over Deuteronomy 24:1-4. The question which opens the dialogue refers to this controversy. "Is it against the Law for a man to divorce his wife on any pretext whatever?" The point of reference is the "Law," and the occasion for this "test" question is the debate between liberal and conservative interpreters of this law. The words: ". . . on any pretext whatever," are an apt description of the liberal school of thought. The Pharisees apparently suspected Jesus of harboring loose attitudes toward divorce and remarriage and they may have hoped to discredit Him on this account.

If such were the case, Jesus' answer must have come as a surprise, although it is now known that He was not alone among His Jewish contemporaries in thinking as He did about the permanence of marriage. The recent discoveries at Khirbet Qumran (the "Dead Sea Scroll Community") indicate that similar convictions were held there among the Jewish Essenes.

I.

On close observation of what Jesus said on this occasion, one can isolate and identify four leading ideas; *these four ideas, I suggest, are central to Jesus' vision of marriage, and foundational for Christian thinking on this subject.*

Like any Jewish teacher of His time Jesus does not present His convictions completely on His own authority. He accepts the point of reference suggested by the Pharisees in their opening question: "Is it against the Law. . .?" In reading the law, however, Jesus focused not where the Pharisees focused, on Deuteronomy 24, but on the creation accounts in Genesis.

1. "Have you not read [His reply began] that the creator from the beginning made them male and female. . .?" With these words, referring to Genesis 1:27, Jesus states His conviction that *human sexuality is a creation of God and part of*

God's original plan for the human family. Far then from harboring an ascetic or antisexual attitude, as it is sometimes thought, Jesus affirmed sexual experience as a good and meaningful feature of human life.

2. "This is why a man must leave father and mother, and cling to his wife. . . ." In these words quoted from Genesis 2:24, Jesus points beyond the mere fact of human sexuality to its goal: becoming free and independent of parents in order that a new social unit might be formed between a man and his wife. Although it is not stated in so many words, the picture here is that of monogamy (one man "clinging" to one wife). The goal, in short, of human sexuality is monogamous marriage.

3. ". . . and the two [he continued] become one body? They are no longer two, therefore, but one body." *We have arrived at the crux of Jesus' marital teachings.* At this point He not only quotes the Old Testament Scriptures, but adds His own words of special emphasis as well. If sexual life is good, and if the goal of sexual life is monogamous marriage, *it is now made clear that the deepest meaning of marriage is that husband and wife become "one body."*

This peculiar term "one body," or "one flesh" as some older versions translate it, will require a few explanatory comments. It is the Jewish way of referring to the profound oneness that is experienced when man and woman become husband and wife through sexual intercourse. The Hebrew word for "body" *(basar)* includes more than is usually thought of by that term today. The body is not the "flesh" as opposed to the "spirit," or the physical as opposed to the soul. "For the Hebrews," writes William Phipps, "a human was not a spirit wearing a garment of flesh; rather, the total self was called flesh." [2]

The union of husband and wife referred to then by the term "one body" includes both the actual bonding of flesh in sexual intercourse, as well as union of mind and spirit, and is referred to in this study as the marital-sexual bond.

4. "So then, what God has united, man must not divide." *With these words Jesus answers the question put to Him by the Pharisees.* They had asked: "Is it against the Law for a man to divorce his wife on any pretext whatever?" Having defined the nature and goal of human sexuality as "one body" in a monogamous marriage, Jesus is ready to meet the challenge put to

Him: "So then, what God has united, man must not divide."
*Do not destroy the psychosomatic unity of husband and wife,
for it is a creation of God.*

There are two crucial points in this concluding sentence.
First, it is remarkable that Jesus can summarize the whole action of man and woman leaving father and mother and becoming "one body" in marriage with the phrase: "what God has
united. . . ." It is obviously the man and woman who themselves
join one another, but God too, it can be said, unites them.
*In and through the very act of forming a sexual bond, God is
seen as working, for it is God who created human sexuality
and gave it this power to unite a man and woman in monogamous marriage.* Notice secondly that Jesus now issues a
command: " . . . man must not divide." Insight leads to prescription! Where a marital-sexual bond of this kind is fashioned,
let no man destroy it!

One may summarize Jesus' opening response to the question
of the Pharisees as follows:

— Sexual life is good.
— The goal of human sexuality is monogamous marriage.
— The meaning of marriage is "one body."
— What God has united, man must not divide.

II.

But the encounter between Jesus and His questioners did not
end there.

"Then why," the Pharisees replied, "did Moses command
that a writ of dismissal should be given in cases of divorce?"
There are certain subtleties here that are worth observing.
In stating their question as they do, the Pharisees speak of a
Mosaic "command." But in point of fact, as already noted,
the law in Deuteronomy 24:1-4 contains no such "command"
specific to divorce.

Jesus then is quite correct when He counters: Moses "*allowed*" you to divorce your wives "because you were so unteachable . . . but it was not like this from the beginning."
Divorce and remarriage are nowhere commanded in the Mosaic
law. The most that can be said is that they are permitted,
and this, Jesus adds, because of "hardness of heart" (literally
cardiosclerosis in Greek). The Jewish scholar David Daube has
caught the thrust of what Jesus is saying here when he wrote:

"Divorce (Jesus contended) runs counter to that complete union between man and wife which God designed when first creating the world. It was sanctioned for a vicious society by Moses, who could only interpose certain safeguards [against unchecked immorality]. But the final community will do without it, in accordance with the original divine plan." [2]

III.

Before summarizing this dialogue between Jesus and the Pharisees, one should yet note its sequel recorded in Matthew's Gospel. Matthew 19:10 ff. tells of a strong reaction by Jesus' first disciples to his marital teachings. "If that is how things are between husband and wife," the disciples are said to have exclaimed, "it is not advisable to marry."

In answer Jesus replied: "It is not everyone who can accept what I have said, but only those to whom it is granted. There are eunuchs born that way from their mother's womb, there are eunuchs made so by men and there are eunuchs who have made themselves that way for the sake of the kingdom of heaven. Let anyone accept this who can" (Mt. 19:11, 12).

There is a long history of interpreting these words in reference to vocational celibacy. According to this interpretation Jesus is speaking here to those who are specially called to renounce marriage altogether. But this way of understanding these verses does violence to their context, where *marriage alone* is under discussion. When Jesus comments, "It is not everyone who can accept what I have said . . ." (19:11) the reference is clearly to the view of marriage just enunciated, not to vocational celibacy. [3]

The words about eunuchs "who have made themselves that way for the sake of the kingdom of heaven," are likewise spoken in reference, not to those who renounce marriage, *but to those who marry and submit to Jesus' radical standard of fidelity, even when it might demand of them complete sexual renunciation* (as in the case of separation without remarriage).

It is this call to unswerving love and loyalty to one sexual companion for life that so astonished the disciples. In a similar challenge, when he warned against material greed, Jesus said: "With men this is impossible, but with God all things are possible" (Mt. 19:26). Jesus did not anticipate that His vision *of marriage* any more than His teaching about wealth, would find

25

acceptance everywhere. The cost of discipleship is high. His words are meant for those who hear His invitation to repent in advance of the coming kingdom of God. They point the way for those who travel with Him in firm faith in God and responsible love for others.

IV.

Perhaps we can now begin to understand why Jesus thought of divorce and remarriage as equivalent to adultery. *Marriage, as Jesus viewed it, is an event of unique oneness between husband and wife. This oneness is no mere human contrivance. It is a creation of God through the sexual bond. Ultimately, neither public law nor religious ceremony can make or break it. The bond of marriage is written into the "flesh" of the persons involved.*

Whether therefore husband or wife commit adultery in the ordinary sense of that term, or divorce and remarry, the effect upon the original marriage is the same. The sexual bond is "adulterated." The inclusive and exclusive emotional and physical union, which is the characteristic of human sexuality as God made it "from the beginning," is sinned against. One destroys what God has created. What God has joined is severed.

When persons are in harmony with the way God made them, their sexual nature will fulfill itself in lifelong marriages characterized by the unity of an enduring sexual bond. Such is the marital and sexual teaching of Jesus. [4]

This teaching captured the early Christian movement, and quickly became a leading feature of its lifestyle. This explains why Paul could so unhesitatingly ask those members of his Corinthian congregation, who were married to non-Christians to remain loyal, even should they have to separate. The marriage bond was seen as so enduring that not even separation or divorce could justify remarriage. 1 Corinthians 7:10 f.

This same attitude is represented in the earliest interpretation of Jesus' teaching on marriage preserved outside of the New Testament canon. In the "Shepherd of Hermas," composed not more than fifty years after the Gospel of Matthew (c. 120), we find the following dialogue:

Q. What shall the husband do if his wife . . . gives way to her passions [and persists in adultery]?

A. Let him dismiss her and remain by himself; if he remarries another he also commits adultery.
Q. What if the wife repents and wishes to return to her husband; shall she not be taken back?
A. Assuredly. If the husband does not take her back, he brings a great sin upon himself; for he ought to take back the sinner who has repented. . . . In this matter man and woman are to be treated exactly in the same way." [5]

It is also worth noting that in calling, as He did, for monogamous fidelity, Jesus brought human sexuality under control in such a way that a new and very joyful freedom between the sexes became possible among His followers. Women and men could once again relate freely as persons in their own right, without fear of destructive sexual affairs. This goes a long way toward explaining the new status of women in the early Christian churches and their surprisingly full participation in the fellowship of these rather intimate groups.

---

1. For a detailed study of the differences between these two accounts and their significance, see David Dungan, *The Sayings of Jesus in the Churches of Paul*, pp. 102 ff.
2. Quoted by D. Dungan, *Ibid.*, p. 121.
3. One of the few really adequate studies of these often misunderstood verses is that of William Phipps in his book, *Was Jesus Married?* pp. 79 ff.
4. David Dungan, *op. cit.*, summarizes the norm as follows: ". . . Jesus . . . really rejects all remarriage and *consequently* all divorce, except when necessitated by adultery." p. 115.
   In answer to the Pharisees, Dungan believes Jesus was saying something like this: "The intention of the Creator is strict monogamy, a single sexual union for each man and woman; your constant divorcing and remarrying is brazen effrontery before God. There should be *no* divorce, unless the marital union is already destroyed *de facto*. . . ."
   "What these Pharisees get from Jesus is essentially a stern denunciation of their sexual vagrancy, holding up against their legitimized lust a view of marriage in which divorce does have its necessary place, but solely as the unavoidable legal consequence of failure at a deeper level of marital kinship." p. 114.
5. Quoted from William Phipps, *op. cit.*, p. 86.

3. jesus' sexual teaching and sexual thinking today

After studying Jesus' sexual teachings in their first century setting, we can now begin relating them to modern trends in sexual life and thought. It is evident that sex standards today are far different from those among the Jews of Palestine in the time of Jesus. In that world, as was noted, the only issue under debate was the question of divorce and remarriage. Today, however, not only divorce and remarriage but a growing list of sex practices, once thought of as perversions, are defended as acceptable patterns of conduct by growing numbers of people. How do the sexual teachings of Jesus formulated so long ago under quite different circumstances relate to these complex modern developments.

This chapter will try to answer that question by first looking at certain general trends in modern sexual thought. Chapter four will focus more specifically on modern thinking about marriage. Chapter five will then summarize the results of this section of study by proposing a set of sexual norms for the period of life from puberty to marriage.

I.

The influences that have contributed to shaping modern sexual thought are of course varied and complex in the extreme. In this brief chapter one can hardly hope to do more than identify a few of the more obvious and important of these. This discussion will focus on two in particular, one a very general influence, that of biological science; the other quite specific: the impact of birth control.

1. Biological Science and Modern Sexual Thought

Certainly any account of contemporary sexual attitudes must take note of *three* major landmarks in modern sexual analysis: first, the sexual theories of Sigmund Freud, introduced at the beginning of the twentieth century; second, the historic research into sexual behavior carried out by Alfred Kinsey and his associates in the 1940s; and third, the recent, widely publicized laboratory experiments into human sexual response by Masters and Johnson. *Dominating all three of these important developments in human sexual self-understanding is a model of man that places primary emphasis on the physical side of his nature and approaches sex predominantly from a biological point of view.*

Although no one of these famous researchers can be held responsible for the widespread present acceptance of this physical approach, yet their work graphically illustrates its effect upon modern man's way of thinking about himself sexually.

Freud, for example, was a medical doctor by training, specializing in neurology before developing his theories of personality disorder. When he discovered that many of the neurotic patients who began coming to him were suffering from unexpressed sexual wishes, he could see this in only one way: as the overly severe repression of a biological instinct. Since this instinct gives pleasure, he began speaking of the "pleasure principle" as a primary human drive and its repression as the major cause of neurosis. [1] Although Freud was by no means the libertine in sexual matters he is sometimes thought to be, the thrust of his analysis was that more leeway should be given to man's repressed drive for sexual pleasure. And this should be done, he argued, under the guidance of human intelligence rather than in bondage to religious rules. [2]

Alfred Kinsey, having first proven his ability in the field of biological research by amassing data on the behavior of millions of gall wasps, also turned to the study of the human species in his later career. Through some 14,000 interviews he accumulated for the first time extensive data on the sexual behavior of North American men and women. While his sex research professed to be purely scientific in that he only wanted to find out how human beings actually behave sexually, undergirding it was a biological instinct theory, assuming that how in fact people do behave is indicative of how they should behave. [3]

Since the major result of his study was to show the rather deviant ways in which surprising numbers of people go about obtaining sexual satisfaction, its impact was to give further support to the notion that sex is a biological function like any other which need not be repressed as severely as it generally is.

It remained however for William Masters and his assistant, Virginia Johnson, to carry this approach to human sexuality to its ultimate conclusion. Because human sexual functioning is primarily a physical response, should it not be studied under laboratory conditions, they asked, with the same techniques and the same care that one follows in the scientific study of other aspects of the human anatomical system? Their answer was to launch a twelve-year research program, in which for the first time sexual activity was brought under controlled scientific observation. From 1954 to 1966, with the help of 694 human participants, they observed under laboratory conditions more than 10,000 sexual orgasms induced by a variety of sexual techniques, including intercourse and masturbation. The results of their research are now being applied therapeutically to growing numbers of persons, married and otherwise, who come to their clinic in St. Louis, Missouri, usually for a two-week period. In addition, their work is being widely publicized through thousands of books, articles, and films. [4]

No event of our time brings more clearly to the fore the physical emphasis in the approach to human sexuality. In their first book-length report on their research findings, entitled *The Human Sexual Response* (1966), Masters and Johnson define sex almost exclusively in terms of what can be recorded by scientific instruments during the various stages of sexual excitement, plateau, orgasm, and resolution, to use their terms. While it is true that they have devoted helpful attention to some of the more obvious psychological aspects of sexual experience in a subsequent publication, *Human Sexual Inadequacy* (1970), their focus remains on the physiology (physical process) of sexual orgasm and its associated pleasure-giving features.

Such a focus encounters the all too obvious fact that sexual orgasm is but one feature of the human reproductive function. It might therefore be expected to have psychological consequences of a very special kind. It is evident, for example, that in the reproduction of the human species the helplessness of the infant at birth and the prolonged period of parental nurture and control necessary before maturity is reached requires a stable family organization. *Were sexual orgasm possible without powerful attendant emotions of wanting to be with the sexual partner and remain together in a more or less permanent way in order to care for the young, the human species would be in grave danger.*

2. Birth Control

However, a second development has intervened to minimize the impact of even such truths as these on modern man's sexual consciousness: the advent of birth control.

The liberalizing impact of birth control on patterns of sexual conduct has been frequently pointed out. *Its importance for altered attitudes toward human sexuality itself is less often noted.* And yet it is at this point, even more than the other, that its revolutionary importance may lie.

Birth control, by artificially sealing off sexual intercourse from its normal reproductive consequences, provides modern man the technology for acting out his recently acquired fantasy to the effect that human sexuality is primarily a physical pleasure in the act of sexual orgasm.

A graphic example of the kind of thinking that can result from such a narrow approach to human sexuality is the popular handbook, *Everything You Always Wanted to Know About Sex But Were Afraid to Ask,* by David Reuben. One looks in vain in this volume for the subjects treated in earlier sex manuals. It says little or nothing, for example, about the reproductive aspects of sex, *except as a problem to be surmounted through birth control.* There is also no discussion here of adultery or fornication. A completely new classification of sexual experience replaces these traditional marriage-oriented categories.

In the opening pages of his chapter entitled "Sexual Intercourse," Reuben tells of three kinds of sex. The first is "repro-sex," or sex primarily intended for reproductive purposes. Of this Reuben has little to say except to disparage it as the main reason for human sexuality. Then there is "love sex." This is sexual intercourse between people who love each other. Of this too, Reuben writes, there is not much need for comment, for "love sex" is, first of all, hard to find, and secondly, where it does exist, sexual difficulties are surmounted easily and one has no need for much advice.

But there is a third form of sex, "fun-sex," and this is the kind that Reuben thinks most people are really looking for. Fun-sex is sex for the pure exhilaration of sexual pleasure. Reuben devotes the major part of his book to this "recreational" use of sex because it is here, he says, where most of the difficulties lie, and tragically so, because as a result people are missing legitimate pleasure.

If one asks what view of human sexuality underlies this amazing classification system, it is obviously the one noted previously. Sex is viewed by Reuben primarily from the standpoint of pleasure in orgasm. Birth control is the technology that makes possible this innocent "fun" without fear of procreation. Needless to say, it is this same sexual philosophy which guides and sustains *Playboy* magazine, which Masters has called "the best available medium for sex education in America today." [5] *The major trend in sexual thinking from Freud to Kinsey to Masters and Johnson, Reuben and Playboy is the emphasis on sex as a pleasure-giving biological function.*

Obviously it is precisely this view of sex that supports the freer attitudes toward extramarital sex so prevalent today. *Where sex is viewed primarily from the standpoint of pleasure in the act of sexual orgasm, just about any and every means for accomplishing this, short of doing violence to another's freedom becomes acceptable.*

II.

Before one turns to the words of Jesus for an evaluation of these trends, it is worth observing that *even from a purely biological standpoint* there are a number of questions that can be raised about such an approach. Birth control, for example, obviously does not erase the fact that sex, in addition to being pleasurable, is a *potentially* procreative act. Regardless of how orgasm is experienced, and whether or not it leads to conception, conception clearly remains a potential goal of this biological function. In orgasm the male produces sperm and/or the female acts to receive them.

Furthermore, it requires no biological sophistication to observe that even in the world of the "lower" animals, this reproductive function takes place within a larger fabric of conduct that not infrequently includes courtship, nesting, and cooperative care of the young. If other members of the animal kingdom, and most especially those primates nearest to human beings possess instincts such as these, are persons to think that there are no similar features associated with human sexuality? *I suggest that it is probable, yes even certain that we do violence to human nature when we imagine that sexual orgasm can be isolated from associated feelings of wanting to live together with a sexual partner, and take mutual responsibility for the young who might be generated by this act. It is, on the face of it, absurd to think that human sexuality can be divided up in this way and treated purely and simply as a matter of orgasm.*

These observations are obviously not unrelated to the insight of Jesus that the human sexual encounter does indeed encompass within itself profound psychological and social features, uniting in "one body" those who experience it as God intended it to be experienced. It is unlikely that the scientific measurements will ever be devised to determine whether or not human sexuality actually is of the monogamous quality Jesus alludes to in His teaching. While the "one flesh" experience does undoubtedly register itself on the neurological system, these finer features of the human psyche almost completely evade the instruments of the scientist.

If, however, wider human experience may be called in as evidence, it can at least be said that monogamy was no invention of Jesus. Jesus Himself based His case for monogamy on the way God created man "from the beginning." This implies that monogamy is woven into the texture of human nature. As a matter of fact, the two oldest civilizations known to man, the ancient Sumerians and the ancient Egyptians, were both monogamous and history does not lack for evidence that this was the case with many other societies as well. In 1934 an Oxford scholar, J. D. Unwin, published a large volume called *Sex and Culture*. In it he examined more than eighty societies with an eye to their sexual practices, and concluded that all the most civilized societies "started their historical careers in a state of absolute monogamy." [6]

The heart then of the conflict between the teaching of Jesus on human sexuality and the one now widespread in the modern world is this: *Modern man, viewing sex primarily from a biological-physical standpoint, tends to reduce sexual experience to the pleasures of orgasm, however achieved. For Jesus, sexual intercourse is an integral part of that event which begins when a man and woman, having reached maturity, leave father and mother, and join together in a lifelong marital-sexual bond.*

1. For an explanation and criticism of Freud's sexual theories by a modern psychoanalyst, troubled by their effect upon modern thinking, see Rollo May, *Love and Will*, 1969, pp. 81 ff.
2. On this point see Freud's *Future of an Illusion.*
3. For an authoritative report on the Kinsey research and its doctrinal presuppositions, see the very informative article by Wardell Pomeroy, Kinsey's close research associate, in *An Analysis of Human Sexual Response*, edited by Ruth and Edward Brecher, 1966, pp. 111-123.
4. For a report on the Masters and Johnson research and its significance, see the book mentioned in the previous footnote, edited by Ruth and Edward Brecher. Also Nat Lehrman, *Masters and Johnson Explained*, 1970.
5. Nat Lehrman, *Masters and Johnson Explained*, p. 168.
6. Quoted from Vance Packard, *The Sexual Wilderness*, 1968, pp. 417 ff. See also the quote from the psychologist Oswald Schwarz at the beginning of Chapter 6.

4. jesus' marital teachings and marriage today

Along with changes toward sex in general have come significant modifications in the modern approach to marriage. Sexual thinking today, as was noted, tends to focus on the physical side of sex and to view it as recreational pleasure. Such tendencies are bound to have a significant impact on the structuring of sexual relations in marriage.

But other equally powerful influences are at work shaping modern attitudes toward marriage. In this chapter these will be identified and evaluated to see to what extent they accord with the insights of Jesus.

I.

One approach to an understanding of marriage today is to take note of *past* images of marriage. These can then be used as a point of reference and comparison. *Following this approach, one quickly discovers three major "models" of marriage that have played a historic role in shaping the institution of marriage as it has been known in Western society during the past millennium.* They are the "sacrament-model," the "contract-model," and the "companion-model." These three models will be described before proceeding to analyze marriage trends today.

1. The Sacrament-Model

Historically the first, this influential model of marriage slowly developed within the medieval Roman Catholic Church and reached its definitive form in the period just prior to and following the sixteenth-century Protestant Reformation. It is the marriage model still dominant in the Roman Catholic Church today, although a process of rethinking is well under way.

Briefly stated, *the sacrament-model views marriage from the standpoint of what happens between man and woman at the time of the wedding ceremony.* The word "sacrament" in the Catholic tradition refers to the gift of supernatural grace or benefit. At the moment of the marriage ceremony, the sacrament or "grace" of a permanent union is granted to the married couple. This sacramental benefit is conferred, not by the priest or minister but by the couple themselves through the exchange of vows. *The marriage ceremony, by means of the exchange of vows, is thus the efficient cause of marriage.* Since only duly baptized Christians can mediate this unique sacrament of marital permanence, a distinction is drawn between Christian and non-Christian marriages. Marriages not formed in this way can be annulled. Once the "sacrament" of marriage is conferred, however, divorce and remarriage are strictly prohibited. [2]

2. The Contract-Model

At the time of the Protestant Reformation, Martin Luther, along with other reformers, directed a strong protest against this Roman Catholic doctrine of marriage. They pointed out that marriage as a sacrament has no basis in the Bible, [3] and secondly, that it is untrue to human experience. Marriage, they said, is obviously not a Christian invention. It exists among all peoples. "It belongs to the order of nature and not to the sacramental system of the church. [4] It is not necessary therefore to have a *Christian* marriage ceremony to have a valid marriage. The marriages of Turk and Jew, Luther argued, are every bit as legitimate as the marriages of Christians.

If that is true, in what then does the true meaning of marriage consist? *Luther's answer was given in his advice that responsibility for marriage should be transferred from the church to the civil courts.* In this advice he shifted the meaning of marriage from a "sacramental-model" to what might be called a "contract-model." Marriage is now thought of primarily from the standpoint of marriage laws rather than religious sacraments. *Marriage is now seen as taking place in and through the contracts made before the civil courts.*

Being contractual, marriage can be terminated, where one of the parties fails to uphold the legal agreement. In this setting then one first encounters the doctrine of the "innocent party." The innocent party is the one faithful to the marriage covenant. From this legal point of view where a marriage partner is *un*faithful, the innocent party may divorce and remarry, for according to the contract-model the marriage ceases to exist when the contract is broken. [5]

3. The Companion-Model

In both the sacrament- and contract-models of marriage, the importance of companionship between husband and wife is never lost sight of. Although the medieval period de-emphasized the sexual side of life, an appreciation for marriage as a deep and supporting friendship nevertheless remained. Luther too spoke endearingly and frankly of the joys of marriage companionship.

But marriage as companionship received special emphasis in the radical wing of the Protestant Reformation, and then increasingly in the English Puritan and Quaker traditions. In the devotion of these earnest Christian groups to a common cause, the wife stood with her husband as a companion in obedience. *Husband and wife complemented and helped one another to fulfill their vocation before God and in doing so they realized together their highest destiny as human beings.*

Where marriages were grossly deficient at this point, they could be terminated. Thus Calvin in Geneva allowed for divorce and remarriage in the event of extreme religious incompatibility. When a Catholic partner would not follow his Protestant mate into exile, Calvin said, the Protestant was free to remarry. The Anabaptist leader, Menno Simons, also permitted separation and remarriage where an unbeliever left his Anabaptist spouse. *Where the essence of marriage is seen to lie in companionship, the marriage is destroyed by major differences.*

II.

But now, in the light of these traditional models of marriage, where is Western man today? Obviously all three of the models discussed continue to exercise their influence on Christians. Although many have ceased to believe in a "sacrament" of marriage received through the exchange of vows, the sacrament-model still has a hold on a person's thinking so long as he views the marriage ceremony as the moment when "marriage" takes place. Furthermore, in spite of a growing number of couples who live together in common-law marriage, the contract-model of marriage is still very much alive and will remain so as long as the civil courts are recognized as having a legitimate concern in the regulation of this vital unit of society.

But it would be hard to deny, I think, that of these three marriage models, the one that is coming to the fore in our time is the idea of marriage as companionship. This at least is the conclusion of a growing number of perceptive sociologists.

Alvin Toffler in his justifiably popular book, Future Shock, has given the most recent summing-up of their conclusions. Love, he tells us, defined as a "beautiful mesh of complementary needs, flowing into and out of one another, fulfilling the loved ones, and producing feelings of warmth, tenderness, and devotion" has become for many in our time the primary purpose of marriage, indeed "the very purpose of life itself." [6] Partners in a successful marriage are said to "grow together," while unhappy husbands often complain that they have "left their wives behind" in terms of social, educational, or intellectual growth. Toffler calls this a "parallel development" theory of love and says it carries the endorsement of marriage counselors, psychologists, and sociologists.

The reasons behind this growing emphasis on companionship in marriage are fairly obvious. In part it is an outgrowth of the modern view of human sexuality, described above, which minimizes the procreative function of sex in favor of its recreational qualities. Even within a more permanent relationship sex takes its place, not as the unique and exclusive bond between these two people alone, but rather as one of many forms of companionship and mutual pleasure, which can be enjoyed interchangeably with a variety of persons.

But the driving urge behind the overriding emphasis on marital companionship, I suspect, is the loneliness and loss of meaning, so much a part of a modern urbanized world. Where primary relations of all kinds have become fragmented, marriage beckons as a haven of interpersonal stability and enrichment.

III.

However, it is proving to be a very fragile haven, and this leads to a final observation on contemporary thinking about marriage. *Where marriage is based on the companion model, it can become vulnerable, as already noted, when this goal is not achieved.* While the reformation sects that fostered this ideal of marriage carefully forbade divorce and remarriage except for major religious or sexual infidelities, the companion marriages in the twentieth century are fracturing on other issues as well.

"Parallel development" of two persons is a difficult achievement under the best of circumstances. Today with life as complex as it is and the life-span so much longer than ever before, the marriage of "companionship" that endures a lifetime is an achievement of the highest magnitude. The faster the rate of change, writes Toffler, the longer the life-span, the worse the odds grow against this kind of marriage. Something has to crack, and "in point of fact," he continues, "something has already cracked — and it is the old insistence on permanence. [7]

"Millions of men and women now adopt what appears to them to be a sensible and conservative strategy. Rather than opting for some offbeat variety of the family, they marry conventionally, they attempt to make it 'work,' and then, when the paths of the partners diverge beyond an acceptable point, they divorce or depart. Most of them go on to search for a new partner whose developmental stage, at that moment, matches their own." [8]

Toffler predicts that more and more people, instead of marrying "until death us do part," will enter into matrimony knowing from the first that the relationship is likely to be short-lived. In the future this may give rise to what Toffler calls a "marriage trajectory" involving a series of three or four marriages in succession as the typical marriage pattern. The first will be a "trial marriage" in the later teens; the second a marriage formalized for the sake of children; the third a marriage for the middle years when the children are raised; and the fourth a marriage for retirement years!

"Serial marriage," summarizes Toffler, "a pattern of successive temporary marriages, is cut to order for the Age of Transcience in which all man's relationships, all his ties with the environment, shrink in duration. It is the natural, the inevitable outgrowth of a social order in which automobiles are rented, dolls traded in, and dresses discarded after onetime use. It is the mainstream marriage pattern of tomorrow." [9]

Such then is the major trend in marriage thinking in our time, one in which older sacramental ideas are virtually discarded and state law is rapidly modified to serve the search for love and companionship in a succession of monogamous partnerships.

IV.

Before relating the teaching of Jesus to these most recent developments in modern life, perhaps a few words of critique should first be directed to those models of marriage, referred to above, which preceded the one now dominant. *Although fashioned in Christian settings, both the Catholic sacramental and the Protestant legal views of marriage leave much to be desired.*

Leading up to the sacramental view of marriage was a long history in the church of downgrading human sexuality. Early in its development Christianity encountered and adopted as its own a form of Greek dualistic thinking which depreciated sexual passion in favor of calm rationality. In this way celibacy came to be valued in the medieval church above marriage, and even within marriage it was taught that sexual intercourse should be confined to the procreation of children. This totally unchristian emphasis reached the stage where even sex for reproductive purposes was thought of as sinful, with forgiveness granted only so that the human race might not die out.

It is this tradition of antisexual bias that forced the medieval church to begin viewing marriage in the nonsexual way outlined above in our discussion of the sacrament-model. While it would appear that this model conserves the concern of Jesus for lifelong marital fidelity, it cannot be too strongly emphasized that it does so in a way that misses completely the meaning of marriage as He taught it. In the sacramental concept of marriage an invisible "grace" has taken the place of sexual intercourse as the core meaning of the marital event. Sacrament has displaced "one flesh" as the essential content of the marriage experience.

The Protestant reformers were surely justified in rejecting this spurious antisexual idea, but they too failed to lay hold of the core of Jesus' marital teaching. *In putting the accent on* marriage as a contract made before civil authorities, they gave insufficient attention to the experience to which that contract leads, namely, the union of man and wife in "one flesh." Lacking this they also failed to grasp the significance of the sexual-marital bond, with the consequence that they too easily equated marriage with any other human legal contract that could be made or dissolved at will.

It can be seen then how the two models preceding the companion model of marriage, have prepared the way for it. Both previous models in their own way *minimize* the place of human sexuality in marriage, the sacrament-model by outright rejection, the contract-model by a misplaced emphasis. This failure to grasp the importance of the sexual bond is now repeated in the companion model, so dominant in our time. *It too does violence to the meaning of human sexuality by treating it as an incidental feature in a series of marital friendships which can be terminated and renewed at will.* Here as well as in the sacrament- and contract-models the magnitude of the sexual encounter in marriage is dangerously repressed.

Thus the meaning of marriage as taught by Jesus stands in judgment of all three of the models of marriage that have dominated Western thinking, and this, surprisingly not because of a depreciation of human sexuality, as so often charged, but because of the awareness of its high significance as the very center of the marital experience.

To summarize: the sacrament-model conserves Jesus' emphasis on the enduring qualities of marriage, but fails to see this as rooted in the sexual event. The contract-model rightly emphasizes the covenant nature of marriage, but again fails to see this as a vital feature of human sexuality itself. And finally the companion-model of marriage accents the deep personal qualities of marriage, but without noting clearly enough how these too are woven together with the sexual bond.

All three approaches to marriage then must be corrected by Jesus' insight that *marriage takes place neither before the altar, nor at the courthouse, nor through a pact of companionship, but in the sexual bond, formed by a man and woman who leave father and mother and join together in "one body."*

How this point of view on sexual teaching might serve as a guide in the formation, celebration, and realization of married life will be the subject of the next chapter.

1. The following survey is based in part on Roland Bainton's excellent treatment of this subject, *Sex, Love and Marriage, a Christian Survey*, Fontana Books, Paperback, 1958.
2. For a thorough discussion of the sacrament-model, see Helmut Thielicke, *The Ethics of Sex*, 1964, pp. 125 ff.
3. In the Latin translation of Ephesians 5:32 the word "mystery" is translated with the word "sacramentum." The reformers rightly pointed out that this gives a false impression of what Paul meant to say. Paul is not saying that marriage is a sacrament conveying a mysterious grace, but rather that marriage is a "mystery" that, properly understood, shines with religious meaning.
4. Roland Bainton, *op. cit.*, p. 90.
5. On the marriage theology of the reformers, see the article by James McEwen, "Marriage and Divorce in the Reformation Period," in *Marriage Breakdown, Divorce, Remarriage*, United Church of Canada, 1962, pp. 72 ff.
6. Alvin Toffler, *Future Shock*, Bantam edition, 1971, p. 249.
7. *Ibid.*, p. 251.
8. *Ibid.*, p. 251.
9. *Ibid.*, p. 252.

5. sexual norms from puberty to marriage

In His teachings on sex, as noted in the previous chapters, Jesus put the accent on its power to unite in "one body" a man and woman mature enough to leave father and mother and become husband and wife. *In doing so, He identified marriage as the goal of human sexuality and human sexuality as the crux of marriage.*

This chapter will explore the bearing of this point of view for the process of reaching sexual maturity, finding a husband or wife, and joining in a marital-sexual bond.

In human beings this process is strongly influenced by sexual norms or principles of right behavior. *Unlike the lower animals where sexual activity is largely under the control of hormones, the sexual life of men and women is primarily patterned by the brain.* [1] This explains why sexual standards are so varied in different civilizations. The anthropologists, Ford and Beach, conducted a survey of sexual behavior in 190 societies and came to the conclusion that human sexuality, to an unusual degree, is a *learned* behavior. [2] Societies *teach* their youth how to behave sexually in accordance with their most deeply held sexual norms.

What approach then will we take to sexual life in the various stages of sexual awakening leading up to and into marriage where the sexual wisdom of Jesus is the controlling ideal? An answer is suggested to this question by focusing on four important moments in this process: puberty, courtship, the wedding, and the marital-sexual bond itself.

1. Puberty

Puberty refers to the signs of sexual maturation that usually appear at around the ages of twelve to fourteen. For girls this is most clearly marked by the first menstruation; for boys, by the appearance of pubic and facial hair and change of voice. Biologically these physical changes announce, not the completion, but a decisive new stage in sexual development. Preparation for sexual life begins at birth and full sexual maturity is not reached until five to seven years after puberty. But at puberty the growing child reaches an obviously critical point in sexual life. The child is no longer a child, but an adult in the sense of possessing a rapidly developing capacity for procreation.

Coming suddenly and unannounced, puberty often arouses anxiety, unless clearly interpreted. *More than at any other time in growing up the child needs an explanation from his elders as to what is happening, preferably before it begins happening.* Undoubtedly this need prompted older societies to fashion puberty rites. These rites celebrated, sometimes in dramatic fashion, the sexual norms and goals of the adult society into which the child was now passing.

Such rituals are notably missing in the more advanced industrial societies, leaving a vacuum which is not always filled. This raises the question, not only as to what sexual norms should be taught at puberty, but as to what agency should teach them. Lacking any strong initiative elsewhere, the public schools seem to be more and more acting as the guardians of puberty instruction in North American society. But for the Christian church to defer entirely to this arrangement may spell defeat at a crucial point. For the schools might adopt the more casual and shallow approach to human sexuality characteristic of modern thinking generally.

In the face of this development Christian families are sometimes singled out as bearing primary responsibility for sharing Christian sexual norms with their children. Let the fathers and mothers, it is suggested, instruct their own children, and not pass this task off to others. But what then should be done, it might be asked, for those children who do not have Christian parents? And furthermore, how many Christian parents are there who know all that needs to be known about the problems facing young people today at puberty? It is a sign of the magnitude of the modern sexual revolution that many adolescents must cope with questions their parents have not yet faced. I mention homosexuality as just one example. But even beyond this, puberty education in the home is difficult, if not impossible, because it is just at this point in life that children often begin to look beyond the home for guidance.

In my opinion then, one of the challenges confronting Christians is to launch sex education programs in the context of the congregation, where a Christian sexual point of view would be shared with every adolescent child, beginning at the time of, or just prior to, the first decisive sexual awakening at puberty.

As to what, more specifically, might be communicated in such a puberty instruction program, the accent might well fall on the following outline, derived obviously from the teaching of Jesus:

A. Sex is good. Value your sexual capacities as a gift of God. Do not be ashamed that you are becoming a man, that you are becoming a woman. These are the things that are happening to you (objective discussion of sexual physiology and emotions).

B. Sex can be misused, just as the body in general can be misused. These are some of the ways sex is misused (objective discussion of sexual abnormalities).

C. The right environment for the expression of human sexuality is a monogamous, lifelong marriage. There are certain experiences in sexual life preparatory to marriage: sexual fantasy, falling in love, courtship, engagement, the wedding.

In short, at puberty youth should be taught to value their sexual nature, to understand and respect the goal to which it is directed, as well as to know what it will take to reach that goal successfully.

2. Courtship

Courtship is referred to here as that stage in sexual development when the adolescent begins to make tentative efforts "to leave father and mother" and to find that person with whom he or she will form a permanent sexual union. It is at this point especially that the older sexual standards have begun to break down. "Nowadays," a recent *Time* magazine reports, "young people begin to have sex earlier than at any other time in U.S. history. . . . The kiss of the 1940s has become the sexual intercourse of the 60s and 70s." [3] In chapter eight these trends and the reasons that Christians should view them with alarm will be explored in detail.

For purposes here one need only note that it was to counteract such trends that the older courtship rituals were devised. *In these rituals courtship was viewed not as a time for sexual experimentation but as a reverent approach to an initial sexual encounter that would give to that encounter all that belongs to it. And this was understood to involve the total commitment of lives in a union that would last for life.* The sexual bond was thought of as so meaningful that it required for its proper realization the careful unfolding of interpersonal relations in several well-defined stages.

First came the "date," the tentative singling out of this girl and that fellow for a specific social occasion together. If the feelings were mutual, a continuing relationship developed, in which the two began to explore in greater depth just who they are and how well they can relate, and all this with sexual restraint. And then came the engagement, in which they professed their love and readiness to make serious and concrete preparations for living together on a permanent basis. But even at this point there was an "escape clause" made possible by the decision not to have sexual intercourse. Finally came the wedding celebration, followed by the first full sexual embrace.

Without saying that these courtship rituals are the *only* right ones, I do not hesitate to suggest that they are an authentic response to that ideal of sexual life taught by Jesus and Christians would do well to defend them until they succeed in devising better ones.

3. The Wedding

In almost all societies a festive celebration marks the transition from courtship to the actual living together of husband and wife in a sexual bond. This celebration is called the "wedding." Like most other issues connected with sex and marriage today, there is a growing confusion about the place and function of the wedding. In some instances it is dispensed with altogether, or reduced to the formalities required by law. In other instances the older traditions are compiled with, but without clear understanding of what the wedding ceremony is all about.

One of the most significant changes taking place in the wedding has to do with the vows that are spoken on this occasion. As some couples face up to their deepest attitudes toward marriage, they begin to question the integrity of the traditional vows of fidelity, "till death do us part." Under the influence of ideas discussed earlier, which envision marriage as a contract that can be broken, or a companionship that can be dissolved under stress, they agree to live together only so long as they love each other.

In the face of these shifting attitudes toward the wedding, two things need to be emphasized:

A. First of all, it should be stressed again that the medieval idea that Christian marriage is an event taking place at the time of the wedding cermony is misleading, as is the idea that the state forms the marriage. While society at large obviously has a legitimate interest in marriages, and there are important reasons for wanting to celebrate them, it should be clear that *neither law nor ceremony constitutes marriage.* The wedding ceremony only does for the persons who are approaching a life of sexual companionship what was suggested earlier is needed at the moment of sexual awakening during puberty. *It interprets ritually what is happening. It structures the approaching sexual encounter in a web of meaning and appropriate emotion.*

B. Seen in this light, it should be clear why the pledge of unconditional fidelity has become such an important part of the Christian wedding celebration. For it is precisely this pledge which says most clearly what Jesus Himself taught about marriage: What God has joined together let no man put asunder. *Marriage vows are made, in the final analysis, not in reference to church sacrament or state law, but in reference to the sexual bond itself, now about to be consummated.* They give public testimony to the fact that this bond will leave the two "no longer two but one flesh." They witness that in this becoming "one body," God is fashioning something new and enduring, and that those so fashioned will respect this new relationship as long as they both shall live. *The moment then in the wedding ceremony when vows of unconditional fidelity are exchanged, more than any other moment in the wedding, pays tribute to the counsel of Jesus that marriage be what God intended it to be: a lifelong union of two people in a sexual bond.*

Needless to say where as much sexual confusion exists as does today, it is all the more important that Christian weddings be conducted in such a way that this vision of marriage be exalted. Couples who dispense with marriage ceremonies, or minimize them, or have sexual relations before the wedding and so destroy the integrity of these ceremonies as celebrations of an approaching sexual bond, weaken the witness of the church in a time when such a witness is most desperately needed.

4. The Marital-Sexual Bond

Where human sexuality is thought of primarily as a biological function, and the sexual event is reduced to "fun sex," all that has been said so far about the stages of preparation for this event will seem ridiculous. And even more ridiculous will be any attempt now to describe the significance of the sexual bond in marriage as the all-encompassing experience it is.

In sex manuals the term "foreplay" is sometimes used to refer to the patterns of sexual stimulation before intercourse. To understand the point of view proposed here, this term might be applied to the whole period from courtship to marriage, and one might think of the sexual event as not just that which takes place on the wedding night, but as the whole process of sexual life that began during courtship and continues through the rest of the lives of those who join as "one body." It is in this sense then that one can expand on the point made several times previously that the essence of marriage is neither sacramental, legal, or companionship, but through and through, sexual.

Human sexuality cannot be compared to any other human experience. It is certainly not to be equated with hunger or thirst, as it frequently is. Without satisfying hunger or thirst a person dies. The human organism does not die without sexual expression. Furthermore, the pleasures of sexual life are not confined to the relief of sexual tensions. Courtship and lovemaking are as much a part of the fabric of sexual joy as the experience of sexual intercourse itself.

This is why, when persons do open themselves to their mysterious sexual natures such persons are brought to a relationship that is permeated through and through with sexual meaning. *Marriage is not just another version of friendship, with sex added. It is sexual friendship in which the sexual dimension radiates everywhere.* The farewell kiss on the way to work, the unexpected call home, the greeting at the end of the day, the words of affection, the whole developing pattern of give and take in body and spirit, as well as the growing art of sexual play in intercourse, all combine to make up that union which Jesus and the Jewish Scriptures call "one body, one flesh."

It is with this in mind that one can say that there is nothing of greater importance to marriage than a sexual harmony in which both partners are growing in their capacity to give and receive sexual love.

---

1. On this point, see Clellan Ford and Frank Beach, *Patterns of Sexual Behavior,* Perennial Library, Harper & Row, 1970, pp. 258 ff.
2. *Ibid.*
3. *Time*, March 30, 1972, p. 59.

6. masturbation

"There is ample evidence," writes the sexologist Oswald Schwarz, "that permanent monogamous marriage is no invention arbitrarily imposed on mankind by ascetic priests or dehydrated moralists, but the expression of what one could almost call an instinct, deeply rooted in human nature. The human species is created that way, and if this were not so, it would be inconceivable that permanent monogamous marriage could have existed everywhere on this planet and ever since the dawn of history as an unchanged form of the relationship of men and women." [1]

The journey of a given individual from puberty to the realization of such a monogamous marriage, however, is a long and sometimes troubled one. On the way are many pitfalls. If one is to know how to relate the teachings of Jesus previously considered not only to trends in modern sexual thought, but to the concrete problems of human sexuality one must look at these pitfalls. One must try to understand, first of all, in what sense they actually are threats to human sexual development, and what attitude to assume toward them.

In speaking of these pitfalls the term sexual "disorder" will be used. By "disorder" is meant that which deviates from an "order" or a "norm." In using these words one accepts that there *is* a norm, a right way of expressing oneself sexually, as opposed to a wrong way.

There is no student of human sexuality, so far as I know, who will not admit to this distinction. Even so libertine an exponent of sexual freedom as Albert Ellis, the author of *Sex Without*

Guilt, is compelled to admit that there are forms of sexual behavior which "the sane and sound individual should normally . . ." avoid. [2] Also David Reuben, whose best-selling sex manual was referred to earlier, while taking a very permissive attitude toward many previously rejected sexual practices, still has his own list of perversions.

The question then is not whether there are sexual disorders, but which sexual practices should be so classified and why. Four disorders in particular have been widely discussed in recent times, with the result that a far more positive attitude is currently being taken toward them than was true even in the recent past. These are: masturbation, fornication, adultery, and homosexuality. In this chapter and the three to follow, each of these perversions, traditionally so called, will be analyzed in order to determine whether a reason does in fact still exist for the historically negative attitude of Christians toward them.

I.

Masturbation is defined as a self-manipulated orgasm apart from a sexual partner. This practice has been observed in very young children, but usually does not emerge as a pattern of sexual conduct until early adolescence. At this time of life it is almost universal for a limited period among boys, less so among girls. The Kinsey research on sexual behavior in the human male discovered that all but 200 of the 5,300 males interviewed, had masturbated at one time or another in their lives. By way of contrast only 58 percent of the 5,940 women later studied by Kinsey had done so. Other studies have shown that the great majority of those who masturbate begin doing so between the ages of fourteen to seventeen.

The emotions associated with masturbatory behavior are varied. It will obviously be impossible to discuss the many facets of this behavior in any great detail. *This chapter confines itself to establishing certain general criteria for evaluating it as a form of sexual expression.*

The importance of doing so is increasingly recognized in current discussions of human sexuality. One recent writer has commented that it is in its attitude toward masturbation that a society begins to shape the sexual mentality of its youth. This comment was made as a prelude to launching an attack on what he feels is the still too prevalent negative posture taken toward masturbation. [3] Brecher argues that the permissive approach to human sexual experience, which he thinks is necessary for a healthy society, can never come about so long as the guilt so frequently associated with masturbation persists.

The argument for a more positive attitude toward masturbation is based for the most part on two points: (1) clinical evidence to the effect that there is no physical harm in the practice, and (2) the fact (revealed in the Kinsey research) that great numbers of American men and women do it without apparent gross psychological damage. Therefore, it angers and mystifies many sexologists that the taboo against masturbation should still be so deep and pervasive. They can discover no reason for this irrational state of affairs than the much-criticized Puritan or Victorian strain in North American culture.

A modification of this outright endorsement of masturbation is represented by such writers as Oswald Schwarz, whose essay, *The Psychology of Sex*, was quoted earlier in this chapter. Schwarz characterizes masturbation as abnormal in childhood, normal during adolescence, and then again abnormal in adult life. As sexual life first awakens at adolescence, the total personality is not yet ready for a mature sexual engagement, Schwarz says. However, the adolescent takes a first step toward sex by *imagining* it. "Masturbation," Schwarz writes, "is a sexual activity in which the contact with the person from whom we derive the sexual stimulus exists only in our imagination . . . solitariness is an essential feature of youth and consequently masturbation is at this age 'normal' because for biological, psychological, and sociological reasons a youth is not yet in a position to have proper sexual relations." [4]

At the same time, Schwarz argues, "If a young man does not overcome this psychic isolation in later years he will not overcome masturbation either. In these cases masturbation is an indication and result of a retarded development, and therefore abnormal. Not a few men never find the way to the other sex, and remain overgrown adolescents all their lives." [5]

II.

In my approach to this sexual practice, I want it to be clear, first of all, that I do not intend to condemn a transient experience with masturbation in the manner of the older sex manuals. In medieval Christianity, where antisexual sentiments were strong and celibacy was the ideal, masturbation came to the fore as a major sin. In this context the evils of masturbation were exaggerated beyond all reason. We can be thankful that today such a distorted point of view is fading.

At the same time I do want to raise certain questions about the blanket endorsement of masturbation as a harmless or even beneficial practice, which is appearing more and more frequently in recent literature. *I would challenge the now widely accepted assumption that masturbatory guilt feelings are nothing but the product of cultural conditioning.* Is it only a Puritan or medieval Christian hangover, one might ask, that feeds the revulsion against masturbation?

A simple observation is surely not out of place here: Obviously human sexuality was not designed for masturbation. And one must repeat the point made earlier, but seemingly all but forgotten in many otherwise sophisticated discussions of human sexuality, namely, that orgasm is by no means an experience in and of itself. It is only one event in the awesome process of reproduction and the human life cycle. Sex, in short, was made for heterosexual intercourse! *On the face of it, masturbation, where the procreative partner is missing, is a highly defective sexual event.*

It should not be marveled at then that this practice triggers such contradictory feelings. *In masturbation that which is meant to be experienced in an atmosphere of deep, psychosomatic unity with another person, in anticipation of parenthood and the founding of a home, is experienced alone.* In masturbation one takes one of the most powerful social agencies of the human body, its capacity for establishing a sexual bond, and turns it into a private pleasure. Is it any wonder then that those who masturbate, adolescents as well as adults, almost invariably feel a sense of loneliness and lack of self-respect after having done so? They have exploited a profoundly significant capacity of the body in a way that is inappropriate to its function and goal. This, it seems to me, is the most obvious and fundamental critique that can be made of this practice. [6]

Along with this observation, however, a number of additional and related criticisms can be made. Orgasm through masturbation must rely, as already noted, on sexual fantasy. This may require for its support pornography or visual stimulation of one kind or another. In developing such a fantasy life, the person who masturbates trains himself/herself to live in the privately contrived and often sexually grandiose world of the imagination, rather than in the real world of experience with another person. Human sexuality becomes for this person a "dream" world in which he or she relates, not to actual persons, but to imagined sexual counterparts. In this way human sexuality is reduced to a pathetic game of "make believe."

In other areas of life where this happens to any significant degree one does not hesitate to diagnose it as a mental disturbance, for one symptom of mental disorder is withdrawal into a mental world of one's own making, where contact with the real world is in danger of being lost. Of course, sexual fantasizing is not usually taken to these extremes, but if persisted in, it can have serious effects on marriage, where this "dream world" may be held onto in preference to the sexual partner. If not the cause in itself of serious mental disorders, it can surely be said that a history of masturbation complicates and makes more difficult the already difficult struggle of many youth for sexual maturity.

On the level of sexual technique masturbation contributes to a highly distorted view of heterosexual life. Masturbation is child's play. It requires no skill, no interpersonal awareness. Anyone can masturbate. But to know how to unite sexually with another in a heterosexual bond that is deeply meaningful to both partners, that is a far different matter. To know how to give and receive in a sexual exchange where the persons involved genuinely love one another is an unfolding art, and one that all too few master, and not infrequently because of selfish attitudes and artificial techniques, conditioned through years of masturbation.

The idea that extensive masturbation is a good preparation for marital sex is, I would say, a new myth being introduced into the sex manuals of today in the name of science, which another generation will have to destroy, in the name of a more mature vision of sexual love.

Measured then against the standard of God's purpose in human sexuality as revealed both in the teachings of Jesus and in nature itself, masturbation must surely be judged an abnormality. Again it should be said, however, that this is not meant as a fear inspiring condemnation of transient experiences with masturbation often characteristic of adolescence. Where however masturbation is retained as a sexual way of life, and even practiced in marital life as a preferred form of sexual experience, it is clearly pathological, and cannot but lead to personal and interpersonal difficulties.

1. Oswald Schwarz, *The Psychology of Sex*, Penguin Books, 1949, p. 218.
2. Albert Ellis, *Sex Without Guilt*, pp. 179, 180.
3. Edward Brecher, *The Sex Researchers*, 1969, p. 318.
4. Oswald Schwarz, *op. cit.*, pp. 42 f.
5. *Ibid.*, p. 42.
6. Havelock Ellis wrote in a similar vein: "The sexual orgasm is normally bound up with a mass of powerful emotions aroused by a person of the opposite sex. It is in the joy caused by the play of these emotions, as well as in the discharge of the sexual orgasm, that the satisfaction of coitus resides. In the absence of the desired partner the orgasm, whatever relief it may give, must be followed by a sense of dissatisfaction, perhaps of depression, even exhaustion, often of shame and remorse." *Psychology of Sex*, pp. 114, 115. Richard Hettlinger, *Living with Sex: The Student Dilemma*, p. 91, quotes this passage from Ellis with approval.

7. fornication

Fornication is the word traditionally used to refer to hetero-sexual relations among the unmarried. It is a word that char-acterizes these relations as immoral. For this reason "fornica-tion" is being dropped from the vocabulary of many, for at no point is the sexual revolution more in evidence than in the affirmative attitude being taken by more and more persons to-ward sexual intercourse before marriage.

The morally laden term "fornication" has therefore been re-placed by a more neutral term, "premarital" sex. In at least one popular sex manual, as already noted, even this distinc-tion is dispensed with. According to David Reuben the basic fact is sexual intercourse, which can be classified in three ways: repro-sex, love-sex, and fun-sex. [1] While ideally, Reuben sug-gests, sexual intercourse should combine all three, fun-sex can be engaged in for its own sake, inside or outside of marriage.

Fornication then, along with masturbation, has been dropped from the "disorder" list by many modern sexologists, and this point of view is now being introduced into school and uni-versity textbooks. One such textbook, for example, *Life and Health*, issued by the publishers of *Psychology Today*, has the following to say about premarital coitus: [2]

"The social and psychological significance of premarital coitus to the individual is linked to social attitudes. In many societies, premarital coitus is expected behavior and serves a useful role in the selection of a spouse. In such societies, there seldom are negative psychological consequences. In societies that condemn the activity, there are possible negative consequences — rejection, guilt, and a greater possibility of exploitation. However, the great majority of American females who have had premarital coitus report that they do not regret it."

This brief paragraph touches on the major arguments that are currently being advanced for freer heterosexual relations among the unmarried. 1. "The social and psychological significance of premarital coitus to the individual," it is being said, "is linked to social attitudes." In other words, the only reasons for negative feelings toward sexual intercourse among the unmarried are *arbitrary* social expectations. There is nothing about premarital sex in *itself* that would call for its prohibition. 2. The proof of this, so the argument continues, is that there are societies where "premarital coitus is expected behavior and serves a useful role in the selection of a spouse." 3. Therefore the only harm that can result from sexual relations among the unmarried is if a society should choose to "condemn" such activity and in this way induce artificial feelings of guilt or rejection. 4. Fortunately, the argument concludes, even in our North American society, where such negative attitudes toward fornication have been in evidence, "the great majority of American females [not to speak of males] who have had premarital coitus report that they do not regret it."

The message is clear: North American young people need have no fear in breaking away from older sex taboos against fornication. They are doing nothing wrong if they engage in premarital coitus and may actually be hurting their chances for a good marriage if they don't.

The extremity to which modern sexual experts, so called, have gone in their arguments for premarital intercourse is graphically illustrated by the writings of Albert Ellis. In his previously mentioned book, *Sex Without Guilt*, after having itemized and refuted fifteen points against fornication, he goes on to list and categorically defend *seventeen* points in favor!

Such concentrated attacks on the standard of premarital chastity have not been without their effect on actual behavior. A poll of sexual attitudes taken in 1970 by *Psychology Today* magazine reveals an overwhelming mood among the middle and upper classes in North American society in support of heterosexual relations among the unmarried. Over 20,000 readers responded to a questionnaire posing 101 questions about all phases of sexual behavior. Regarding attitudes toward premarital sex, the magazine reports: "Left to P. T. readers' discretion, virginity in pursuit of virtue would be a vice: fewer than one out of ten advocate chastity until marriage. . . . And the majority agrees that premarital sex often equips people for more stable and happier marriages." The report adds, *"Psychology Today* readers act on their attitudes: about 75 percent of them have had — or were having — premarital relations." [3] Another recent survey of adolescent sexual behavior has confirmed these statistics. Johns Hopkins demographers Melvin Zelnik and John Kantner, after studying the sexual habits of 4,611 teenage girls, reported that 14 percent of the 15-year-old females they questioned had experienced intercourse, and that the percentage rises rapidly beyond that age: 21 percent at age 16, 27 percent at 18, and more than 46 percent at age 19. [4]

In the face of these overwhelming trends toward premarital intercourse, can a defense still be made of the attitude that fornication is indeed a sexual disorder?

I.

Although the general approach to answering this question will now be familiar to those who have read the previous chapters, it is not wasted time to try once more to grasp this problem in the light of Jesus' teaching, for it is only as this teaching is made specific that one can discover whether it does in fact provide some help for the journey through the contemporary sexual wilderness.

Looking at the various ideas offered in support of sexual intercourse before marriage, there are two in particular that would seem to merit some further discussion. The first is the belief that negative attitudes toward fornication are nothing but *cultural* reactions without foundation in the act of fornication itself. The second is the increasingly widespread dogma that there do in fact exist societies where premarital sexual activity is approved and practiced, with beneficial results. It is by questioning these two assumptions that the reasons will begin to emerge for looking at fornication as a disorder.

First, what can be said about the assumption that fornication is wrong only because a culture says it is wrong? Strangely, the prejudices in modern society are running so strong just now in favor of a more permissive approach to premarital sex that all attention is focused on those societies where fornication is approved conduct. Very few sexologists are studying those societies that put restrictions on such activity, or asking why in fact they do so. That one cannot lightly reject the anthropological evidence on *both* sides of this question is amply demonstrated by such cross-cultural studies as those of Ford and Beach *(Patterns of Sexual Behavior). Of 189 societies for whom information exists, approximately one third wholly disapprove of premarital and extramarital relations, and an even larger group takes what Ford and Beach call a semi-restrictive attitude (disapproval, but without severe sanctions).* [5] In addition to these there is a significant group of more permissive cultures. Before one makes a too quick choice in their favor, *it is worth asking why the restrictive societies take the approach they do.*

A strictly anthropological answer to this question may not be possible, but two quite obvious facts about human sexuality that somehow keep getting lost in many modern discussions have a bearing on the subject at hand. The one fact is that sexual intercourse, whether premarital or marital, has to do with the reproduction of the species. This remains true, whether or not birth control is practiced. The reference here is not to the mental intent of a particular act of sexual intercourse, nor to the question of its value apart from procreation in the formation of a marital bond, but only to the obvious fact that it is by this means that the human species reproduces itself. Surely this places it in the category of one of the most awesome acts of which men and women are capable, and in itself should explain in part at least why many societies take a negative view toward careless, promiscuous behavior in this regard.

But even more important and just as obvious are the psychological dimensions attendant upon sexual bonding. As was suggested earlier, there is evidence that monogamy is written into the fabric of human nature. In any case, it is clear that in human beings the young require an unusually long period of care before they can become self-sufficient, and during this period need the sustained attention of both a mother and father. That powerful emotions should operate between those who unite sexually, binding them together psychically so that they will form a stable family unit for the sake of the young, is certainly to be expected *and it would be tragic for the human species were such psychic emotions missing.*

Taking these two facts into account, there need be little wonder that many societies have tried to help their youth restrict themselves against a sexual life that would weaken their capacity for those more permanent sexual bonds that are so obviously necessary for the healthy reproduction of the species. To do so is surely not an arbitrary act, but one that is rooted in the nature and goal of human sexuality itself.

But what then is to be said of those societies where this is not the case? Here again a word of caution is in order. The assumption that a more permissive attitude toward premarital sex is without adverse consequences is surely in need of more careful study.

As an example I cite a recent report of sexual practices among a small group of people living on the South Pacific Polynesian island of Mangaia. [6] The author of this report describes in detail the rather free heterosexual relations that exist there. Mangaian girls, he tells us, are not only allowed, but encouraged to have sexual relations with a number of boys before marriage, and the boys, for their part, soon after puberty, are trained to engage in sexual intercourse by older, experienced women. Prior to marriage they may have had sexual relations with a dozen or more girls, and even after marriage, there are no strong sanctions against extramarital affairs.

This all sounds somewhat like the sexual world toward which we are moving in North America. But is it a really good world? So far as the Mangaians are concerned, the author seems to think so, but he does not hide the fact that there are certain problems; two in particular.

One of these, as might be expected, is the considerable amount of extramarital infidelity that prevails in this society. In addition to the general looseness of sexual standards, two specific reasons for this high rate of extramarital activity are given. One is the belief that married couples, if temporarily separated, continue to need a sexual outlet and are therefore justified in finding it where they can. Another even more significant cause of infidelity is the Mangaian girl's strong inclination to return to the first man "she enjoyed sexual intercourse with." This latter observation illustrates graphically the powerful hold of a primary sexual bond, even where its importance is apparently unrecognized by societal mores or structures.

An additional flaw in this sexual paradise is the disturbing fact that "the Mangaian male is subject to *tira*, a condition that ranges from an initial period of insatiable desire to a final stage in which he cannot achieve an erection." The author of this study seems baffled by this phenomenon. He suggests that it may be a "biological penalty" which the Mangaian male must pay for his sexual activity rate. But it is virtually certain that impotence is a *psychological* "disease" rooted in defective sexual attitudes. [7] It is far more likely then that we should trace this peculiar defect in Mangaian sexuality to their having isolated sexual experience from its proper setting in the human psyche: the faithful love of husband and wife.

The comments thus far are intended only as a warning against falling too easily for the current attitude that sees premarital sex as harmless in itself, and looks for supporting evidence in those societies where fornication is practiced freely and with supposedly happy results.

II.

To turn now, in a more direct way, to Christian teaching on this subject, Jesus said that a man and woman, reaching maturity, and joining sexually as husband and wife, should remain faithful to the sexual bond that unites them. Jesus first gave this teaching, as we have seen, in defense of His negative attitude toward divorce and remarriage. What bearing does it have on fornication as a sexual practice?

It may seem strange that Jesus Himself did not speak more explicitly or extensively to this particular question. It should be remembered, however, as noted earlier, that He had no need to, for the simple reason that the Jewish community never raised it. Among the Jews of Jesus' time there was a firm standard against sexual relations among the unmarried. According to the Jewish Scriptures, in fact, a young man who engaged in sexual relations with an unbetrothed girl had to marry her, and remain married for life, without the right of divorce. Deuteronomy 22:29. In "The Testament of Simeon and

Judah," a Jewish tract dating from approximately 100 BC, we read: "Beware . . . fornication, for fornication is mother of all evils. . . . Beware . . . for these things withdraw you from the law of God, and blind the inclination of the soul, and teach arrogance, and suffer not a man to have compassion upon his neighbor. They rob his soul of all goodness."

It is also well known how this same highly negative attitude toward fornication permeated the first Christian churches. Paul, for example, lists fornication, along with idolatry and sorcery, as among the sins that decisively cut people off from the kingdom of God. See Galatians 5:19 and Colossians 3:5 f.

Even though Jesus Himself then had little to say explicitly against premarital sexual relations, there can be no doubt as to where He stood on the matter. His contemporaries and His first followers all taught against it and His own teaching implies a point of view toward human sexuality that clearly excludes it.

But now once more, precisely why? Why this highly critical stance that would brand fornication a disorder? By sexual "disorder," it is worth repeating, is meant a departure from the norm, something that aborts the real intent of human sexuality. If fornication is a sexual disorder, it must be so because the persons involved do violence to their sexual nature and to the sexual event itself. In what sense, more precisely, can fornication be said to do that?

The fornicator fails to respect the depth and permanency of the relationship that is always potential in heterosexual intercourse. [8] *Where a man and woman are open to what is really happening in sexual relations, they become aware of a powerful psychosomatic bond being fashioned between them. The fornicator represses this side of the sexual experience for the sake of sexual pleasure.* In doing so he inflicts a wound on the sexual sensibilities of himself and his partner, a wound that can result in total loss of sexual function.

We have already noted an example of this in the Mangaian study referred to above. Prostitution affords another well-known illustration of the same crippling process. It is common knowledge that the prostitute often scorns the persons who visit her, and can maintain a sexual way of life only through a complete sterilization of her sexual feelings. With the advent of promiscuous heterosexual relations among young people in society in general, it is sometimes said, that the role of the professional prostitute is no longer sought or needed. It might better be said that this trend is contributing to sexual prostitution as a mass cultural phenomenon. This will mean not the enhancement of sexual pleasure in the long run, but its end. If anyone doubts this, let him ponder the growing number of books already on the market dealing with sexual impotence, or see the explicit film, "Carnal Knowledge," which traces with commendable candor the sexual disintegration of a college fornicator.

Contrary then to the opinion of many, the Christian opposition to fornication is not rooted in an antisexual bias, but in an awareness of what is needed for the sexual side of human nature to reach maturity. The value it attributes to the monogamous sexual bond is a sign, not of prudery, but of appreciation for the height and depth of all that is there to be experienced when a man and woman leave father and mother and become "one flesh."

---

1. David Reuben, *Everything You Always Wanted to Know About Sex*, pp. 53 ff.
2. *Life and Health*, CRM Books, 1972, p. 217.
3. *Psychology Today*, July 1970, p. 42.
4. See the report in *Time*, May 22, 1972.
5. Ford and Beach, *Patterns of Sexual Behavior*, pp. 115 and 194.
6. "Too Much in Mangaia," by Donald S. Marshall, *Psychology Today*, February 1971, pp. 43 ff.
7. The reader is referred to our discussion of "impotence" in the "sexual therapy" sections of our study.
8. On this point, also see Paul's line of argument in 1 Corinthians 6:12-20.

8. adultery

Adultery, like fornication, is a word laden with negative emotions. It refers to sexual infidelity on the part of those who are married. Until recently in the Western world this was ranked among the worst of sins. As fornication was thought of as deviant sex *before* marriage, so adultery was looked upon as illicit sex *after* marriage.

As with fornication, however, so too the negative attitudes toward adultery are being modified. The word itself is beginning to disappear from our vocabulary. Just as "premarital" sex is taking the place of the term "fornication," so "extramarital sex" is increasingly being used in place of "adultery."

Adultery means literally "to adulterate," to "add to" in such a way as to weaken or destroy. Applied to sexual infidelity among the married it implies a moral judgment. These infidelities "adulterate" the marital bond by adding something to it that threatens it. By dropping the word adultery from our vocabulary in favor of the term "extramarital" these negative connotations are avoided, and we are well on the way toward rethinking the sexual conduct appropriate to married life.

Further evidence that such "rethinking" is indeed going on is not hard to come by. Already in 1948 Kinsey reported to an astonished North American public that by the age of forty 26 percent of the married women and 50 percent of the married men questioned had had extramarital intercourse. In the *Psychology Today* survey conducted in 1970 and quoted in our previous chapter, [1] 40 percent of the married men, the majority of whom were not yet thirty, and 36 percent of the married women of the same age-group, had already engaged in extra-marital relations. Only one in five of the 20,000 polled thought such affairs were wrong under any and all circumstances.

These statistics again reflect the position taken by many leading modern sexologists. A recent collection of essays, entitled *Extra-marital Relations*, edited by the president of the American Association of Marriage Counselors, Gerhard Neubeck, [2] includes among its articles a polemic by Albert Ellis which outlines six "healthy" reasons for extramarital relations. "The good Judeo-Christian moralists," Ellis writes, "may never believe it, but it would appear that healthy adultery, even in our supposedly monogamous society, *is* possible." [3]

Gerhard Neubeck himself, the editor of these essays, seems to agree. In a final summation he writes: "Forsaking all others has never been a realistic expectation, and, based on the assumption that there always will be others, couples can explore what the possibilities for themselves and each other should be: when, where, and how the additional individuals can be incorporated into the basic and nourishing unit." [4]

A popular marriage manual, written by anthropologists George and Nena O'neill, weaves advice of a similar kind into its portrait of the ideal modern marriage. Their book bears the descriptive title, *Open Marriage*, and actively opposes the "smothering togetherness" of what they describe as the more traditional "closed marriage."

As to sex in the "open marriage," they write:

"Sexual fidelity is the false god of a closed marriage. . . . Fidelity, in its root meaning, denotes allegiance and fealty to a duty or obligation. But love and sex should never be seen in terms of duty or obligation, as they are in closed marriage. . . . In an open marriage, in which each partner is secure in his own identity and trusts in the other, new possibilities for additional relationships exist, and open (as opposed to limited) love can expand to include others. . . . These outside relationships may, of course, include sex. That is completely up to the partners involved." [5]

That the thinking of the O'neills is no quirk of a small *avant garde* is indicated by its presence in the school text referred to in chapter seven. "Marital infidelity," they write in the CRM textbook, *Life and Health*, "is a frequently useful modification of the marriage contract. . . ."[6] America's middle-class, puritanical society has long held that infidelity of any sort is impossible if one truly loves one's mate and is happily married, that any deviation from fidelity stems from an evil or neurotic character, and that it inevitably damages both the sinner and the sinned-against. . . . [But] recently, sex researchers have examined the unfaithful more representatively and have come up with quite different findings."[7]

It is apparent then that those who would defend sexual fidelity as normative for married life and classify "adultery" as a sexual disorder will be increasingly hard pressed to do so.

If adultery is sin, as the Christian church has traditionally said, on what basis can one continue to uphold this point of view in the face of the growing number of onslaughts against it?

It is important at this point to again become as precise as possible as to the meaning of marriage, for in discussing adultery, marriage is presupposed and "marriage" can be viewed from many different angles. Not only must one reckon with various models of monogamous marriage, as noted in a previous chapter, but with various forms of nonmonogamous marriage, such as polygamy, serial monogamy, trial marriage, group marriage, and the like. *It is apparent that adultery cannot be defined in relation to each and every one of these marriage concepts or forms and retain an identical meaning in each instance. What one society, for example, may call adultery in reference to its marriage definition another will structure as "a second wife" (polygamy), and still another as "a second marriage" (serial monogamy). Also in a situation where couples live together sexually on a "trial" basis, but refuse to legalize their relationship, a subsequent "official" marriage might be a "first" marriage from one point of view, "adultery" from another.*

Furthermore, in speaking of marriage in the ceremonial or legal sense, one must take into account that a given marriage may somehow be so defective as to disqualify as a marriage. Inability or unwillingness of husband or wife to unite sexually, for example, even though legally and ceremonially united, is grounds for annulment in almost all societies. In a not dissimilar sense marriages are sometimes contracted with such partial commitments and such defective attitudes that the more appropriate term for these relationships could well be "fornication." It is apparent that in such cases adultery cannot literally be understood as "adulteration." Such marriages have nothing to adulterate.

To understand adultery then, one must again refer to the marriage standard given in the teaching of Jesus, and not only there, as has been repeatedly said, but in creation itself. When we speak of *adultery as a crime against our sexual nature, it is with reference not just to any notion of marriage, ceremonially or legally defined, but with reference to that profoundly deep and meaningful bond that the Scriptures call "one flesh."* Where persons are mature enough to leave father and mother, love and respect a wife or husband, and join in a sexual bond, something happens so deep and so enduring that it can only be said that "they are no longer two, but one body." *It is only with reference to this ideal of marriage, that we can take proper measure of the nature of adultery.*

And seen in this light its significance is, as has been suggested, to adulterate, to weaken and, if persisted in, to destroy this primary sexual bond. Adultery is an act of violence. It ruptures the tissue of experience binding husband and wife together. The pain that ensues is experienced as "jealousy." Marital jealousy is no artificial emotion, but only the other side of that profound feeling of inclusiveness and mutual loyalty essential to the marital-sexual bond.

The adulterer then is on the same dangerous and destructive journey as the fornicator. He is guilty of assaulting his own sexual nature, that of his partner, and the one with whom he commits adultery. By isolating sexual intercourse from the feelings of fidelity and total self-giving associated with it, the adulterer or adulteress destroys a vital dimension of the sexual experience itself and ultimately some of the highest and finest aspects of human personality. Adultery, as with all sexual disorders, is a form of personal, social, and finally sexual suicide.

In any case on this point there can be no doubt as to the mind of Jesus. His explicit counsel to married men to guard, not only against adulterous actions, but adulterous thoughts (Mt. 5:27 ff.) is well known and thoroughly consistent with His high vision of what marriage is really all about, as expressed in those texts which are the recurrent theme of this study.

Before concluding this chapter, however, it may be worthwhile to return again to those arguments for adultery which are being aired more and more today and to note one thing

especially about the context in which they are being put forward.

*The point being that marriage as an institution is and will
suffer a shift in meaning where promiscuity is as widespread
as it now threatens to become in North America.* In this light
it should come as no surprise when adultery too takes on a
different connotation. If premarital sex becomes the order of
the day, this already weakens the capacity for entering into a
truly meaningful marital-sexual bond. Add to this an indulgent
sexual fantasy life, stirred not alone by pornography, but by
the constant barrage of sexual stimulation in so-called respec-
table magazines and movies, not to speak of the growing homosexual emphases invading our culture, and it should be apparent that growing numbers of people will come to marital
sexuality already jaded and far from ready to realize that
deeply unifying bond that is the sexual goal.

The result inevitably will be the down-playing of the sexual
side of marriage, which we already see taking place, with the
continuation of an "adulterated" sexual style along the lines
prepared for in premarital life. *Marriage in such a context, as
already noted in chapter four on that subject, will become increasingly just another form of friendship or companionship
with "sex" an added but by no means exclusive feature of it.*

Perhaps some indication of where marriage is headed in
North America can be seen in the following description of the
Kaingang tribe in Brazil. The description appeared in an
anthropological review of marriage practices:

"Once a couple are married they do not drop the liaisons
formed before marriage. Their long training in philandering
and the absence of an ideal of faithfulness have not suited them
to the stability that marriage implies. Furthermore the absence
of binding legal forms or big property stakes, as well as the
knowledge that a meal can always be found at one's father's or
brother's fire, that one's mother or sister-in-law is ready to cook
the food and spread the bed, makes marriage brittle and its
rupture is not sharply felt. Yet in an utterly contradictory manner, the Kaingang believe that a man and woman, once they
are 'sitting together,' belong to each other. . . . This theoretical
possessiveness comes into constant conflict with the actual sharing
in which the young people have taken part all their lives. The
young man, who for years before his marriage has dallied with

the wife of anyone from his father to his second cousin, who has day in and day out enjoyed adultery with an equally delighted adulteress, decides suddenly, when he is married, that his possession should be exclusive. 'I left my wife,' Yuven told me, 'because she took Kanyahe and Kundagn as lovers. She sleeps with everyone. All the women are that way. When their husbands go away they sleep with others. That is why I want to marry a Brazilian woman.' " [8]

It is worth noting that the "utterly contradictory" feelings between premarital conduct and postmarital expectations, referred to in this description, seem still to be very much in evidence among us as well. In spite of the modern emphasis on sexual freedom, there is no indication of a diminishing search for marital stability, no matter how often frustrated. Perhaps one might point to these marital expectations in the midst of sexual chaos as "remnants" of that monogamous instinct, which, as was suggested, is written into the fabric of human nature. Even promiscuity of the kind being experienced today in North America seemingly cannot eradicate these monogamous intuitions completely.

But it *is* possible that the darkness of the sexual wilderness might deepen, before light breaks through, pointing in a new direction. It is my conviction, of course, that such light has already broken in, if persons but knew it and were ready to be guided by it. It is the light of Jesus' brief but penetrating insight into the meaning of human sexuality. And in this light Christians would do well to continue to walk, not only for their own sakes, but as a witness to God's will in a time of destructive confusion.

---

1. *Psychology Today*, July 1970, pp. 39 ff.
2. *Extra-marital Relations*, ed. by Gerhard Neubeck, Prentice-Hall, 1969.
3. *Ibid.*, p. 161.
4. *Ibid.*, p. 198.
5. Nena O'neill and George O'neill, *Open Marriage*, 1972, pp. 256 ff.
6. *Life and Health*, CMR Books, 1972, p. 296.
7. *Ibid.*, p. 297.
8. *Extra-marital Relations, An Anthropological Review of Extra-marital Relations*, by Gerhard Neubeck, pp. 123 ff.

9. homosexuality

Homosexuality refers to sexual relations between individuals, male or female, of the same sex. The term derives from the Greek word "homo" meaning "same." The word "lesbian" is sometimes used in referring to female homosexuality exclusively.

It is only in the last several decades that open discussion of homosexuality has become possible, and there is still much confusion in the minds of many as to its nature, causes, or consequences. Here too a debate rages as to whether it should be classified as a disorder.

On this point homosexuals themselves have begun to take the initiative. In many urban centers homosexual colonies have organized in defense of their right to acceptance on a level with heterosexuals. Within the Christian churches themselves the age-old strictures against homosexuality are being challenged. The mass media have given publicity to homosexual congregations, where homosexual marriages are solemnized by homosexual ministers, and numerous publications by Christian authors have defended homosexuality as a valid and fully acceptable way of life. [1]

However, attitudes toward homosexuality among professional counselors who work intimately with homosexuals are by no means uniformly positive. In contrast to the more liberal views that have gained ground in recent times toward masturbation, fornication, or adultery, the approach among many psychologists and psychiatrists toward homosexuality remains cautionary, if not outrightly negative.

But before pursuing further the reasons for these attitudes, I will try to summarize what is now known about homosexuality.

I.

It was again Kinsey who first called the attention of North American society to the extent of homosexual behavior. His research indicated that at mid-century there were some two or three million Americans with homosexual tendencies, about three fourths of them men, and one fourth women. According to the statistics of the Institute for Sex Research of Indiana University "about 4 percent of all white males are exclusively homosexual all of their lives." [2]

Although many assume that homosexuality is on the increase, as yet there is no way of knowing whether this is true or not. Homosexuality is certainly more visible, and the probability of an increase is high. It is not unlikely in fact that a link exists between the general deterioration of sexual standards and the incidence of homosexuality in a given society. The epidemic scale of male prostitution and homosexuality in Rome just prior to its decline is the best known historical example. [3]

But what is the cause of this turning of sexual desire toward someone of the same sex? Because homosexuality is more prominent among men than women, for the sake of brevity, this question will be answered in relation to male homosexuality. Many of the contributing factors to male homosexuality, of course, are similar for female homosexuality as well.

In tracing causes we must first of all make certain distinctions as to types of homosexuality. There are degrees of intensity in homosexuality as there are in heterosexuality. Perhaps homosexual tendencies exist in all persons at some stage in life. Children, for example, during preadolescence go through a "buddy" period. Also outward circumstances might more or less force homosexual interests upon a person whose emotions are basically heterosexual. This can happen in artificial one-sex societies, such as prisons or armies. Homosexuality under such circumstances may be occasional, marginal, and transitional.

The following comments on homosexual causation do not have this type of homosexuality in mind, but rather what D. J. West calls "obligatory homosexuality." In obligatory homosexuality the homosexual tendency is deeply rooted. Strong attractions toward those of the same sex exist regardless of the external circumstances. [4]

Two points now are fairly well established as to the causes of this type of homosexuality. First, "There is increasing agreement among authorities in the field that genetic, constitutional, or glandular factors play little role in the causation of homosexuality, whereas psychological, social, and cultural factors do play key roles." [5] In short, homosexuality is not a physical but a behavior disorder. It is not inherited or "caught" but learned as the consequence of growing up in a disturbed social environment. What then are the social disturbances that contribute to homosexuality?

This leads to a second, now generally established point as to the origins of this disorder: a contribution to homosexuality is a disturbed parent-child relationship — especially the combination of a seductive or overattached mother and an absent, weak, or rejecting father. This is not to say that this is the only influential factor. "It becomes increasingly clear," says Evelyn Hooker, head of a task force on homosexuality for the National Institutes of Mental Health, "that homosexuality is an extraordinarily complicated phenomenon, in which the causative factors are multiple."

She continues, "Among these are: inappropriate identification with the opposite-sexed parent; fear of, or hostility to, either parent; reversal of masculine and feminine roles in parents; cultural overemphasis on the stereotype of 'masculinity' which produces feelings of inadequacy in males who are not able to fulfill this expectation; rigid dichotomy of male and female social roles with failure to allow for individuals who do not easily fit into either of these; and easier access to sexual gratification with members of one's own sex in adolescence, resulting in habit patterns which persist." [6]

However of the many contributing causes, the key factor seems to lie in the parent-child relation. "Whatever the exact truth of the matter," writes D. J. West in a summary report on homosexual causation, "a large amount of evidence exists to show that the circumstances of child-rearing have particular relevance. Males who have had a combination of a dominating, possessive, sexually prudish mother and a weak, absent, or aloof father risk developing sexual difficulties in general and

72

homosexual orientation in particular." [7]

What seems to happen in such a child-parent situation is that the mother succeeds in binding the son to herself in such a way that he is in a competitive relation to the father. This leads to confusion in his achieving a masculine identity. At the same time his intimate relation to the mother requires that he block off his normal masculine sexual feelings toward women, because of the powerful incest taboos at work.

Homosexuality then, of a compulsive and obligatory kind, is brought about to a significant degree by mothers who choose a favorite child in preference to their husbands, and who weave a bond between themselves and that child that is pseudo-marital.

When this is understood, one can also see a connection, alluded to above, between the general loosening of sexual standards in a given culture and the rising incidence of homosexuality. In a rootless and alienated society, when through sexual promiscuity marriages are weakened, the numbers of mothers without faithful, sustaining husbands inevitably increase. This fact contributes significantly to the general insecurity of these mothers. In rearing their children they may turn to them for the intimate relations lacking in their marriages. Where a son is involved the situation is ripe for an overly intense incestuous bond (latent in every mother-son relation). The outcome is often homosexuality.

I submit that homosexuality may therefore be described as the sexual plague of a monogamous society gone promiscuous. Those societies that sow the winds of heterosexual freedom, ironically, reap the whirlwind of homosexual perversion.

II.

But can one so glibly say that homosexuality is a perversion, a disorder? At the beginning of this chapter it was noted that questions have been raised on this score, with homosexual behavior being defended both by homosexuals themselves as well as others, including Christians.

Certainly an important distinction needs to be made between homosexuality as a social crime, punishable by fines or imprisonment, and homosexuality as a mature or immature, good or perverted form of behavior. That society is revising its attitudes toward the punishment and virtual banishment of consenting adult homosexuals is certainly to be welcomed. Whatever one might think of homosexuality as a way of life, it is probably no worse than many other disorders afflicting the human race, which for that reason are not made the object of public trial and punishment.

But that homosexuality is in fact a disorder, it would appear hard to deny. Homosexuality simply goes against the most obvious function of human sexuality. If sexual life is anything, on the face of it, it is a part of the human life cycle. It engenders powerful feelings of mutual responsibility in the nurture of a new generation. It unites a man and woman in a powerful bond that becomes the nucleus of a new social organism, the family.

In homosexuality the act of orgasm and the powerful emotions associated with it are violently torn loose from their normal psychic setting. The homosexual encounter is a pathetic game of mutual masturbation. As with any such gross misuse of function, disturbances result. In this instance the disturbances go to the depth of psychic life. That is why homosexually bound persons are generally such profoundly unhappy people. Fortunately, with increased understanding of the origins of this unhappy condition has come also a more hopeful outlook for therapeutic change for those willing to seek it. What may be involved in such therapeutic change, not only where homosexuality is concerned, but in the case of the other sexual disorders as well, is the subject of our next chapters.

---

1. A particularly striking example is a collection of essays entitled *The Same Sex*, ed. by R. W. Waltge, Pilgrim Press, 1969.
2. Quoted from *Sexuality and Man*, compiled and edited by the Sex Information and Education Council of the United States, 1970, p. 74.
3. All too ample documentation of the homosexual state of affairs in Rome just prior to its fall is offered by Raymond de Becher, *The Other Face of Love*, 1969, pp. 55 ff.
4. D. J. West, *Homosexuality*, Third edition, 1968, pp. 33 ff.
5. *Sexuality and Man*, p. 78.
6. *Ibid.*, p. 78 f.
7. D. J. West, *op. cit.*, p. 264.

10. general considerations

The previous chapters have set forth a set of sexual ideals, based on the insights of Jesus. These ideals were explored in relation to sexual thinking in modern times, and a number of sexual disorders, traditionally so-called, were examined. This discussion will, I trust, have begun to indicate the outlines of a Christian approach to human sexuality and the extent to which it is in conflict or harmony with trends in North American society.

The task of a Christian, however, would only be partially realized were he to conclude the study at this point. More is needed than a sexual ideal or a description of sexual failure. One must also address himself to the question of healing for those who are sexually disturbed. What is to be done where someone has gotten lost in the sexual desert? What approach is to be taken where sexual sins have already taken their toll?

This section then will discuss strategies of healing for sexual disorders where the Christian ideals outlined above are the guiding insights. In doing this, I would hope to avoid both "legalism" and "cheap grace," two attitudes toward the sexually "fallen" that have been recurrent in Christian history. *Neither harsh rejection nor superficial acceptance will answer to the deep needs of those who have become enmeshed in sexual sins.* What is needed is a healing strategy that knows something about sexual disorders and what must be done to initiate a process of restoration.

Needless to say such an approach is consistent with Jesus' attitude toward "sinners." It will be remembered that on one occasion He pointedly compared His mission to that of a physician. Mark 2:17. Those who are well, He said, have no need of a doctor, but those who are sick. And to these He came not simply with comfort, but with the prospect of help.

It is in this framework, in fact, that Jesus' specific words about human sexuality are best understood. As previously noted, His saying on divorce and remarriage is not so much law as the wisdom of a knowledgeable physician. Jesus does not so much tell us what should or should not happen in divorce and remarriage, as warn us as to what in fact *does* happen. "Whoever divorces his wife and marries another, commits adultery. . . ."

Also His statement about the meaning of marriage and the command, "What God has joined together, let no man put asunder," is no arbitrary legislation, but the prescription of one who knows what is necessary for the psychic and spiritual health of mankind.

Jesus' sexual teachings then give not only a sexual norm, they also offer guidelines for sexual healing. In taking these teachings and seeing to what extent they do in fact help us in the face of specific sexual problems, several general principles should be kept in mind:

1. Sexual disorder, like any other "illness," it should be remembered, may progress to a point beyond healing. This is only another way of saying that sexual sins may have consequences that cannot be corrected. Christians have no quick, easy solutions to all problems, any more than others do. They, like everyone else, must face up to the limits of what can be accomplished by way of healing in this imperfect world. For the final answer to many of the problems and questions that trouble us, we must look forward beyond the boundaries of this life, threatened as it is by sin, decay, and death.

2. It must also be emphasized that even where the prospect of sexual healing exists, caution may need to be exercised in approaching sexual problems of a particularly severe and complex nature without recourse to the specialized knowledge of those professionally trained for work in this area. The discussion that follows is certainly not intended as an answer to any and all sexual disturbances, but only as an indication of the direction in which help and healing may be found, given the ideals discussed in the earlier chapters of this book.

3. When speaking of sexual healing, it is well to keep in mind that sexual problems, by and large, are not physical in origin, but psychological. They are rooted in the mind and will, the heart and soul. This is why an aspect of healing in this area may, and often must, include an appeal to the capacity within us to make decisions. "If your right eye should cause you to sin," Jesus said, "tear it out and throw it away. . . . If your right hand should cause you to sin, cut it off and throw it away . . ." (Mt. 5:29 f.). These urgent words are not meant, of course, literally. They speak rather to our latent power to decide. While sexual therapy may include more, it will seldom include less than an appeal to change, while change is still possible.

4. But a Christian healing strategy is by no means "repentance therapy" alone. The Christian call to change is always made in firm faith that ". . . God is at hand." Even before man "turns," there is a benevolent Father-Spirit turning toward him.

Several modern psychologists have discovered this reality outside of the context of Christian faith and have tried to express it in nonreligious language. Rollo May, for example, tells us of a very deep and wholesome "intentionality" (sense of purpose) that wells up in his patients as they open themselves to the truth about themselves. [1] Victor Frankl speaks of "meanings" that come breaking in upon his clients as they turn away from their narrow self-preoccupations. [2]

While then Christian sexual healing calls for decision, it also proclaims the gift of unexpected help to those who turn in the right direction. This, in part at least, is what Christianity means by "grace" and "forgiveness" — the generous offer of pardon and constructive assistance in the face of sin and failure. It is at this point that one might speak of Christian prayer as a wellspring of healing.

5. But again, a Christian strategy of healing does not rely alone on gracious help from God. Ideally it also offers the "turning" and "repenting" individual a healing and helping community, the church, where through open, supportive dialogue the "stronger" bear the burdens of the "weak" and "so fulfil the law of Christ" (Gal. 6:2). Sexual sins are difficult to cope with alone. The guilt is often too strongly felt, the emotional conflicts too complex. But through sharing with others

who genuinely care, their disturbing power diminishes as from the lips of friends are heard encouraging words of guidance, challenge, consolation, or forgiveness as the need may be.

6. Finally (it should be said again) sexual function, in a given individual, is dispensable. Man does not require this function to live. He does not even require it to live well. A Christian approach to sexual healing, therefore, does not hesitate prescribing the termination of sexual activity where its pathological continuation endangers the whole personality. "It will do you less harm," Jesus said, "to lose one part of you than to have your whole body go to hell" (Mt. 5:30).

With these general considerations before us we are now ready to turn to a selection of specific sexual problems, to see to what extent a Christian approach can offer some guidance.

Needless to say the suggestions presented here can at best be no more than a beginning in the discussion of this subject. My only hope is that those counseling with sexually troubled persons, not to speak of the persons themselves, may find some of them helpful and perhaps be stimulated to test, correct, and expand on what is only touched on here.

The analysis will focus on two major topics: (1) sexual healing for the married, and (2) sexual healing for the unmarried.

---

1. See the analysis of will, wish, and intentionality in Part II of Rollo May's book, *Love and Will*, 1969.
2. Frankl has written extensively on the "will to meaning" which he postulates as a fundamental attribute of being human. See especially his book, *Man's Search for Meaning*, first published in 1959, now available in paperback (Washington Square Press, 1963).

11. sexual healing
for the married

This section refers to those who are "legally" married. In earlier chapters of marriage it was emphasized that legal marriage may not necessarily correspond to marriage in fact. According to the insight of Jesus, the crux of marriage is a monogamous sexual bond ("one flesh"). Where such a bond exists, marriage exists, whether legalized or not. If such a bond does not exist, or exists in a poorly realized way, and yet the persons involved are legally married, this will be called a defective marriage in need of sexual healing.

From this standpoint and terminology sexual healing for those who are married will be approached. *In diagnosis and therapy of the sexual problems of the married, it is suggested the crucial issue is the quality of this monogamous sexual bond.*

With this in mind two major problem areas emerge: (a) problems in a marriage where the monogamous bond has been defectively realized and (b) problems in a marriage where the monogamous bond has been realized with someone outside the legal marriage.

A. Problems in a marriage where the monogamous sexual bond has been defectively realized.

Admitting that this one chapter cannot begin to treat this large topic adequately, I can only hope to illustrate some of the ways in which the insights gained in the previous analysis may be of value in helping those troubled by marital-sexual problems. Remarks will be confined to three of the most obvious sources of difficulty in such marriages: (1) emotional ties to the parents, (2) promiscuity before marriage, and (3) promiscuity after marriage. I will then comment briefly on the possibility of divorce and remarriage as a way out of marital-sexual difficulties.

(1) Emotional ties to the parents

One of the most frequent and troublesome causes of defective sexual experience in marriage is an overly intense emotional bond between a husband or wife and the parent of the opposite sex. The discussion of homosexuality has already indicated how this is a factor in male homosexuality, where the emotional tie with the mother is almost always extraordinary. When such men marry, the wife is pressed into the role of a mother substitute. The husband seeks to reproduce in his relation to his wife the relationship he had with his mother. Since the sexual side of the relation to the mother had to be repressed, the same happens in the marriage. Sexual intercourse between husbands with this disorder and their wives is often defective to an extreme degree. While fantasizing a homosexual relation, the husband may simply use his wife as a convenient object for masturbation. This has nothing to do with marital love, and it should be obvious why, in spite of being legally married, the wives of such marriages are profoundly frustrated and unhappy, and feel themselves to be something less than wives.

But even where the tie to the parent of the opposite sex is not so intense as to produce an outright homosexual disorder, it may be close enough to form a disturbing competitive element to the marriage. The relation between father and daughter or mother and son may continue to take priority over the bond between husband and wife. Where this is the case it cannot be said that the man and woman have really "left father and mother." Yes, they may have gone from the parental home physically, but inwardly they are not really free to become "one flesh" because they are still bound to their parents.

But even subtler and more disturbing things can happen in such instances. Where a father or mother forms a special relation to a son or daughter, they inevitably introduce into the personality of their children some very distorted ideas. By singling out the child in this way, they convey the idea that they prefer this child, not only to other children in the family, but to the husband or wife. For the child so chosen this is a heady experience, and a profoundly disturbing one. At a time in life when the son should *be* a son, and the daughter a daughter, they are made to feel like husband and wives, and this in competition with their own fathers and mothers! The son grows up feeling superior to his father, the daughter better than her mother. A profound narcissism (self-fixation) is the result, often accompanied by an excessive superiority-inferiority complex.

Children growing up in such circumstances frequently become loners. The world is beneath them. It does not recognize their greatness and worth. Therefore too bad for the world — they will go it by themselves. But that too is an unsatisfactory way of life. So they seek out those people, rare though they be, who will recognize their special worth. More than likely this is the type of person they will marry. Then husband or wife are forced into the role of the adoring and pampering father or mother. This, of course, is an impossibility and as a consequence such marriages are fraught with difficulty, as already suggested. Sexually too there is always a shadow, for in the emotional bond to the mother or father sex had to be repressed. The more the marriage takes on the shape of that prior parent-child relationship, the more it disintegrates sexually and in every other way.

The problem must be dealt with, first, by frankly facing what is going on. The tie with the mother and father must be broken. But this of course is not simply a matter of "leaving" home, but of turning away from the distorted mental outlook built up through this relationship. The son or daughter must climb off the pedestal where he is something "special." A whole new way of life must be fashioned sexually and otherwise, built on giving and receiving love. This, of course, is easier said than done. It may require many personal and interpersonal crises, not to speak of the wise counsel of knowledgeable friends or professional counselors.

Speaking specifically of sexual intercourse, steps will need to be taken to affirm it as the good that it is through loving that concrete person who is the wife or husband. Grandiose sexual fantasies must be set aside and all pampering of such fantasies through pornography. In their place the needs and concerns of the particular husband or wife will come to front and center.

One sign of progress will be *mutual* fulfillment in sexual intercourse. Here the work of Masters and Johnson may be affirmed in their recent publication, *Human Sexual Inadequacy*, in that they outline some of the steps that can be taken to overcome difficulties in sexual intercourse. Sexual orgasm is not the be-all and end-all of sex, but sexual relations without orgasm on the part of both partners is also (I would say obviously) a defective form of sexual life. This not being a marriage manual the subject is not enlarged upon here. I would however recommend that married couples who want to enrich their sexual experience read the description of marital sexuality found in the book by the Catholic couple, Joseph and Lois Bird, The *Freedom of Sexual Love*, to name only one example. Sexual love in marriage is an art, and one that the married have no excuse for not mastering, given the educational resources now available.

(2) Promiscuity before marriage

By promiscuity is meant all forms of random sexual behavior, whether masturbation, heterosexual petting, prostitution, or fornication. The effects of this kind of conduct on the formation of a monogamous sexual bond have already been described in the discussion of sexual disorders in chapter seven. For this reason comment will be confined here to a summary, with special reference to what may be necessary for overcoming the consequences of these defective experiences. Problems resulting from premarital promiscuity can be identified under two headings: (a) repression of sexual emotions, and (b) immature sexual function. Both problem areas will be commented on and the directions suggested in which an answer might possibly be found, always bearing in mind of course the general considerations mentioned earlier.

a. Repression of sexual emotions

"Repression of sexual emotions" refers to the dangerous narrowing of focus that takes place where sexual experience is sought primarily for pleasure. In this narrowing, as has been repeated, the deeper feelings of wanting to generate a child, of wanting to build a home, of wanting to be and remain "forever" in unity with the sexual partner are pushed aside. It is now being recognized that the upthrust of such repressed feelings is one reason for the frequent failure of promiscuous women to practice birth control.

Rollo May has written graphically of this repression of sexual emotions in his book *Love and Will*. He speaks there of modern girls who are "victims of a gigantic repression in them-selves and in our society — the repression of eros and passion and the overavailability of sex as a technique for the repression. . . . The assumption that the ultimate goal of existence is the satisfaction of impulses has led sex into the cul-de-sac [dead-end street] of tedium and banality." [1]

To win back sexual emotions pushed aside in this way requires an act of understanding and will. Just as the person emotionally tied to the parent must "leave" that parent, in the inward sense described above, so persons bound by a history of promiscuity must radically "forsake all others" in order to be truly and deeply available to their wives and husbands. In promiscuity we not only repress sexual emotions, we scatter them. To be healed sexually we must gather them back and give them to the woman or man with whom we are married.

b. Immature sexual function

Promiscuity not only leads to the loss of some of the finer aspects of sexual experience, it inevitably leads to some very deficient, one might say, childish sexual practices. A shallow egotistical form of sexuality inevitably leads to its mechanization.

In men this mechanization may result in what is termed "premature ejaculation" and eventually impotence. Premature ejaculation may reflect a pattern of promiscuity where the goal was not, of course, genuine love of another, but simply quick, often secretive and guilt-ridden self-gratification.

Impotence may also result from this same self-indulgent syndrome, although the causes vary. A man intent on his own sexual pleasure at any cost will increasingly discover that this pleasure is very dependent on his feelings of "manhood." But promiscuity presents many threats to such masculine feelings. Lacking the atmosphere of mutual love and respect normal to sexual life, sexual doubts easily intrude into promiscuous affairs, if guilt has not already done so. The man begins to question his sexual potency. Complete failure of sexual function may result.

In women this is called frigidity. The causes are similar, except that in women promiscuity may take its toll even more quickly and decisively. The reason is that "the feminine woman gives much of herself in the act of lovemaking with a strong emotional involvement. . . . The feminine girl, who gives herself completely to a boy she loves, expects a permanent relationship and finally marriage."[2] If then a woman should decide to engage in sexual relations without love and commitment, this quickly leads to guilt, and scorn of the sexual partner. Frigid sterilization of all sexual emotions is the result.

The answer to these problems of immature sexual function is not, then, in the first place, some new technique, but rather pressing forward in the decision to build a loving, faithful marriage. In the wake of this decision new techniques will surely follow. The quick, selfish sexual encounters learned through promiscuity will be put aside in favor of "courtship" patterns where the emphasis is on open communication and mutual give and take in a growing love relationship. In such an atmosphere sexual life will begin to emerge as a vital part of the growing together of two into one, body and mind. Again I refer to the book by Joseph and Lois Bird (mentioned earlier) for instruction as to what a truly loving sexual encounter might look like.

(3) Promiscuity after marriage

It hardly needs to be said that if promiscuity before marriage has a negative effect on the formation of a meaningful monogamous bond, this is obviously even more the case after marriage. And yet one encounters promiscuous sexual practices even among husbands and wives dedicated to monogamous marriage, with apparently little awareness of their detrimental effects.

I refer particularly to masturbation and an adulterous fantasy life. It is not unusual, I have discovered, for husbands who masturbated extensively before marriage to continue to do so afterward. The same is true for both husbands and wives in the area of adulterous fantasies. In one instance I counseled a couple where the wife had entertained an extramarital fantasy for a period of some five years.

These marriages and these persons of course are often found to be struggling with problems other than these particular sexual deviations. In some instances these practices are associated with still unresolved parental ties of the kind discussed above. But whatever their genesis, they compete all too obviously with the fashioning of a meaningful marriage and will need to be terminated before a solid marital bond can be realized.

I sometimes compare the approach advocated here to that taken by Alcoholics Anonymous to the problem of the "next drink." In AA all aspects of the alcoholic problem are dealt with. But while this total therapy is in progress, there is one piece of advice applicable to all at all times: Stop drinking! In the same way, although it might be argued that promiscuous practices of the kind mentioned here have deeper roots, the practices themselves can, if properly approached, be terminated, and usefully so, while these other difficulties are being explored and dealt with. As to what we mean by a "proper approach," reference is again made to the "general considerations" previously mentioned in chapter ten.

(4) What about divorce and remarriage?

In the light of the discussion of Jesus' teachings in earlier chapters it might seem that the answer to this question is a foregone conclusion, at least so far as the Christian is concerned. Did not Jesus say that divorce and remarriage are equivalent to adultery, and is not adultery clearly wrong?

Jesus' statement on this question, however, as also was noted, was made in reference to a marital goal, the leaving of father and mother and becoming one flesh. It is to this event that He referred when He spoke of "what God has joined together, let no man put asunder."

In defective marriages however it is precisely this that has not happened, or at least has been experienced in a marginal or unsatisfactory way.

One cannot avoid then asking the question whether the legal arrangements that tie two people together, where a deeper psycho-sexual bond was never realized, should compel them to stay together. *If in fact a married couple was never really "joined together" in a meaningful sexual bond, does it make sense to say, let no man separate them?*

The answer is evident in those cases where the legal marriage was not followed by sexual intercourse of any kind. Both church and society have recognized in such a state of affairs unquestioned grounds for legal annulment.

In reality, however, even where sexual coupling takes place the experience may be of such a distorted and disturbed kind that it is tantamount to "no intercourse at all" or even worse. The extreme example of this of course would be rape. Are there situations where the struggle to achieve sexual healing is a hopeless struggle, and the lives of both persons involved would be better served by terminating the relationship?

Obviously to raise this possibility opens the door to all manner of specious arguments and false conclusions. Not to raise it however may result in a needless torment for persons otherwise capable of living a worthwhile human existence. In saying this I am thinking, for example, of women married to men crippled by a serious homosexual disorder.

In the following section a "counseling" approach is advocated for the complex problems of those who are divorced and remarried. The same is necessary, I would suggest at this point. Only with careful attention to what in reality has and is happening in the marriage, and especially to the psycho-sexual bond, can valid judgments be arrived at.

In general where Christians are involved every effort should be made to build the marriage, in spite of the sexual inadequacies that may plague it. Husbands or wives, however, who will not or cannot take their role in forming a meaningful sexual bond should recognize that this will threaten the marriage at its foundations. The Apostle Paul apparently had a similar point in mind in his rather straightforward advice to married couples in his Corinthian congregation. 1 Corinthians 7:3 ff.

B. Problems in a marriage where the monogamous sexual bond has been realized with someone outside of the legal marriage.

Even more troublesome and difficult than legal marriages where the marital sexual bond has been defectively realized, are legal marriages where one of the persons in the marriage may be sexually "bonded" to someone else. By sexually "bonded" is referred to that relationship which Jesus spoke of as "one flesh." These persons, for whatever reason, left the persons they were united to in this way, and married someone else. But the original monogamous bond still retains its powerful psychic hold on them.

This of course is only another way of describing what can happen in divorce and remarriage, where the initial marriage was authentically "one flesh." It also describes what can happen when persons who live together sexually, without legalizing their relationship, separate and marry someone else. In both instances, adultery is the result, in the sense described earlier. Those who unite sexually in a loving way and then separate and marry someone else, adulterate their oneness, Jesus said, and human experience confirms the truth of His words.

The Christian church has traditionally taken a legalistic approach to this pattern of conduct. The words of Jesus were thought of as "law" in a sense similar to that of the laws of the state. When Christianity triumphed as a state religion, the "law" of Jesus was in fact, in some instances, codified as the law of the state. More recently, with the decline of state religion and the weakening of cultural Christianity, Christian oriented legal norms are increasingly rejected and Christians are now often found taking their cues as to the right approach to divorce and remarriage from laws being fashioned by modern secular societies.

The comments that follow will try to illustrate another approach, based on the realization (outlined in the previous sections of this study) that Jesus' marital teachings are not so much law as "wisdom." He does not so much legislate as prescribe in the context of certain insights into the nature and meaning of human sexuality.

With this in mind, this discussion of divorce and remarriage will first sketch a general approach and then outline several alternative courses of action that might be taken, depending on the circumstances.

1. General Approach

Two principles bear reemphasizing: First, the inadequacy of civic law as a final guide to marital status and second, the decisive importance of following instead what might be termed a Christian "counseling" approach.

In approaching the first principle, Christians might do well to recall how little experience they have had in North America with living in conflict with their social and civic environment. Generally they have assumed that the laws of the state will reflect and support the ideals of the Christian majority.

This expectation may now work against those who would follow Jesus' teachings on marriage, for it has left them vulnerable to the shifting laws of a state on its way to becoming more and more secular. A striking case in point is modern marriage legislation. As divorce and remarriage laws are liberalized everywhere in the Western world, Christians will be hard pressed to fall in line with these changing legal definitions of marriage. And yet to do so may in many instances compromise the marital wisdom for which, through the centuries, the church has been custodian.

To understand what is at stake in this confrontation in the West between Christians and civic ways of defining marriage, it might be useful to recall the recent encounter between the Christian mission and polygamy in Africa. Polygamy, of course, until recently was as deeply rooted in the African cultural and civic heritage as serial monogamy (one marriage after another) now threatens to become in North America.

And yet the church could not adjust to polygamy and remain true to its own marriage ideals. A conflict was inevitable. As a minimum, unmarried converts were asked to reject polygamous expectations and to confine themselves to monogamous marriages. A controversy developed over what to do with polygamous marriages already contracted. Some suggested putting away all wives but one; others advised only against adding additional wives. The only point to be made here is that the church could not make peace with a polygamous vision of marriage, no matter how weighty the legal and social traditions that sanctioned it.

I suggest that the tension is no less acute today between the Christian mission and legalized serial monogamy in North America. If the church simply concedes to the patterns of divorce and remarriage prevailing in the culture, viewing everyone who gets their sexual relations legalized as legitimately married, it will not only betray its Lord, who so directly challenged precisely this superficial way of thinking in His own time, but it will betray those involved as well. For it is in the name of love and of reality that Jesus spoke His sharp words against the adulterers of His generation who thought that they could make legitimate their callous sexual conduct by legalizing it.

But what approach then *should* be taken? I suggest a counseling approach. [3] By this we mean one that sympathetically and yet realistically gets at all the facts, and advises contextually in the light of them. In a counseling approach it is not enough simply to look at wedding certificates. One must look into lives, discern experiences, and work out solutions in the face of specific circumstances.

As an example I cite a young couple contemplating marriage. They first met each other while at the university and during a courtship of more than a year formed a sexual bond in anticipation of becoming legally married. Instead, however, the man broke off the relation, went to another part of the country, and married someone else. That marriage terminated in divorce. It was then that this couple found each other again, both realizing that the bond between them since university days was one that could not easily be broken, and had in fact been in effect through the intervening years.

The marriage they now contemplated would be looked upon by law and society as a "second" marriage. As the facts came to light in counseling, it began to look more like the restoration of an earlier nonlegal "marriage" after several years of infidelity.

The sexual biographies that present themselves to a counselor today are of course not always as uncomplicated as this one, and even with counseling it will be difficult to know what course to suggest. At points like this all the perspectives mentioned in chapter ten may need to be brought to bear on the situation, and especially prayer to God for guidance and help.

2. Alternative Possibilities

In order, however, to make as concrete as possible the approach being suggested, several rather focused alternatives will be spelled out. These should be referred to only as examples of the types of solutions that might be indicated where the legal and the psychic-monogamous attachments are in genuine conflict.

Obviously these comments are conditioned by the social situation in North America at this time. For this reason polygamy is not discussed although this too, in other cultural settings, might be considered the "lesser of two evils" under some circumstances. [4]

a. Terminate the legal marriage

Although such a strategy may seem questionable at first glance, it is common knowledge that there are legal marriages where the law is only a thin cloak for adulterous conduct of the most flagrant kind. The Bible itself affords two examples of this type of perversion: Herod's acquisition of his brother's wife Herodias (Mt. 14:2 ff.), and the man in Paul's Corinthian church who was living (no doubt legally) with his stepmother (1 Cor. 5:1 ff.). It is well known how John the Baptist lost his life because of his straightforward criticism of Herod's conduct, and Paul's reaction to the Corinthian affair was equally strong. There are situations where "legalized adultery" is the only proper term for what is transpiring and termination is the only truthful and right course of action.

b. Terminate the legal marriage in favor of the original monogamous marriage

Again in some instances marriages of a deep and long-standing nature have been abandoned for affairs that are only too obviously adulterous. Had a legal process of divorce and remarriage not taken place, and were these persons not for this reason accredited in the eyes of society as married, there would be little question as to the right course of action.

But legalizing an adulterous affair does not (as has been said now many times) fundamentally change the picture. When the facts are known it may become clear that a given legal marriage should be terminated to make way for reestablishing the original and actual marriage.

c. Build the legal marriage into the best marriage possible under the circumstances

In multiple marriages events may transpire which make either of the two previously discussed alternatives difficult, if not impossible. Children may be involved in ways that would call in question terminating the present legal marriage. Furthermore, even though the "second" marriage is "adultery" for one of the partners, it may not be for the other. For the second wife, for example, this may be the first marriage, as deeply binding to her as it was for the original wife.

Once relations of this kind are established it may be impossible to turn back. The only course of action is to "stay as they were before God at the time of their call" (1 Cor. 7:24) and make the best of it. Then the approach will be to build the legal marriage, in spite of its flaws, into the best marriage possible under the circumstances.

In this case all that has already been said about realizing a meaningful marital bond would apply. The painful thing however is that in this instance "forsaking all others" will have to include the original husband or wife. This of course is what already began to happen when the husband first left his wife and began entertaining the thought of a new sexual relation, or when the wife first left her husband. Every act of adultery is a destructive blow against the original monogamous union. In these actions a person is doing what Jesus said should not be done, violently severing what God has joined together. In forming a second marriage this work of destruction may need to be brought to completion.

In summary, sexual healing for the married requires a sharp focus on that monogamous bond that Jesus and the Jewish Scriptures call "one flesh." For those legally married who have not experienced this bond deeply, because, let us say, of emotional ties with the parents, or promiscuity before or after marriage, therapy lies in facing up to the distortions wrought by these deviations, in turning away from all competitive loyalties, and in actively building the marriage, seeking there the strengthening of that bond now imperfectly realized. Divorce and remarriage should come into question only where it is clear that the marriage is so defective that a marital sexual bond neither exists nor, in all likelihood, ever will.

For those who have experienced such a monogamous bond, but with someone other than the person with whom they are legally married, the options would seem to be either to terminate the legal marriage and remain single, or to return, if possible to the person with whom the monogamous bond was originally formed. Circumstances however may call for the preservation of the legal marriage in spite of its defective quality. In that case, it will need to be built, as in any marriage, on the principle of "forsaking all others," including, in this instance, the original wife or husband.

In conclusion, it should be emphasized again that for all our sins and errors, there is forgiveness and help as soon as we are ready to reach out for it, and yes, long before. This may not always release us from the consequences of our mistakes, but it will enable us to begin moving in a healthy and ultimately hopeful direction.

1. Rollo May, *Love and Will*, 1969, pp. 70, 87.
2. Fritz Kant, *Frigidity: Dynamics and Treatment*, 1969, p. 20.
3. For a perceptive treatment of this approach and its problems, see Walter Trobisch, *My Wife Made Me a Polygamist*, 1971.

4. I am indebted to Walter Trobisch, *Ibid.*, for this suggestion. In his book he indicates how a counseling approach might help the church in dealing with polygamy in Africa.

12. sexual healing
for the unmarried

It is surprising and discouraging to discover how little has been written about the sexual life of the unmarried. In the large library to which I have access, I discovered shelf after shelf of books on sexual matters. Virtually all of them treat the subject from the standpoint of marriage. I could discover scarcely any that had anything to say specifically and explicitly about the sexual life of the unmarried.

And yet this issue cannot be bypassed. It is all too apparent that many single people must find a way to live with their sexual potentialities unrealized, not only in the normal time of maturation before marriage, but for an entire lifetime. It is also apparent that in the present age, flooded as it is with sexual stimuli and confused with unclear standards for unmarried sexuality, more and more single people are getting involved in sexual practices with which they do not know how to cope. What does a Christian healing approach, such as the one outlined in this study, have to say to such persons?

As an initial step to formulate some kind of an answer to this question, I will offer some comments about celibacy as a way of life. Then in order to illustrate more specifically what it might take to live celibately a discussion of therapy for masturbation will follow. Finally, corrective approaches to premarital sexual intercourse and homosexuality will be explored.

A. Celibacy as a valid way of life

Celibacy refers to a life without marriage, that is, a life without any active expression of the sexual function.

It is well known how the Christian church already in the

third and fourth centuries began to value celibacy as a way of life superior to marriage. By the twelfth century the Catholic Church was requiring celibacy as a condition for the priesthood and, although debated, that is still the case today.

Protestant Christians for their part returned to what seems the more original Judaeo-Christian point of view toward celibacy, that it is a valid way of life with certain advantages, but is certainly not to be ranked above marriage.

Today, however, Christians seem to be moving one step further. Celibacy is now viewed as virtually impossible. Those who through no choice of their own are deprived of marital sexual experience are often looked down upon with pity. Perhaps one reason for the silence of both church and society on the question of the sexual life of single people is the unspoken agreement that the older sexual codes that deprived them of sexual experience are simply unworkable.

In the face of this embarrassed silence, I offer a few tentative points of reference, more as a way of opening the conversation than of concluding it.

1. The foundation of any sound approach to celibacy as a way of life must be built on the awareness that human beings do not need, of necessity, to give expression to their sexual function in order to live, or even to live well. It is not required of men and women that they engage in sexual relations or that they experience that bond called marriage. In this sense one can say that sexual function is not one of the "vital" functions. Without it no one dies, although it would be folly to deny that its loss deprives a person of something profoundly meaningful.

2. It is equally important to recognize that *misuse* of sexual function offers no real alternative to its proper role in human experience. If we are correct in saying that human sexual experience requires a loving monogamous bond as the context for its realization and maturation, then there can be no substitute for that. To seek sexual substitutes with prostitutes, or in homosexuality, or through masturbation will in the long run only make matters worse and never provide a meaningful alternative to marriage.

3. Denial of sexual function is a possibility. The myth of irrepressible biochemical sexual drives is just that, a "myth." As noted earlier, sexual function in human beings, in distinction from animals, is largely regulated by the mind. By adopt-

ing a certain mental attitude the sexual side of life can be actively diminished. Obviously in a promiscuous world this task is not easy. It should be remembered however that this is a challenge not alone for the unmarried, but for the married as well. Some further comments on this score will follow in the discussion of masturbation.

4. Recognizing the possibility, desirability, and even the necessity of celibacy, where marriage is out of the question, one needs to be equally candid about the deprivations and handicaps, as well as the special challenges and opportunities of such a life. The unmarried no less than the married need to talk to each other, need to learn from and challenge one another, and together fashion a set of coping strategies and life-style norms for their special circumstances.

This does not mean that married and unmarried should form separate communities. On the contrary both can contribute a great deal to each other. But just as married couples have found it useful to share in special marriage enrichment seminars, so I would hope that the time will come when Christian celibates might also feel open and free enough about their life situation to get together in a similar way for frank discussion of their life as single adults.

Among the topics to be considered along this line might be: the art of building warm, close, ongoing, interpersonal relations; avoiding the "old maid" syndrome; avoiding the "bachelor" syndrome; being feminine without marriage; being masculine without marriage: the advantages and disadvantages of being single.

In short, celibacy as a valid way of life is greatly in need of some fresh thinking, especially among Protestant Christians, where the opportunity of an "ordered" life for single people has been a glaring community weakness. Whether there is support or guidance for such a fresh look in the words of Jesus, or elsewhere in the New Testament may be open to question (see above, pages 25 ff.). There can be little doubt however that Jesus Himself was celibate, and still less that others throughout the Christian movement from its earliest days (1 Cor. 7) have seen in celibacy, not so much a tragic deficiency to be pitied, as a special opportunity for loving service on behalf of God and His coming kingdom. The churches and the world would indeed be poorer if it were not for dedicated celibate men and women who are able to give of their time and energies in special ways for others, precisely because of their freedom from family responsibilities.

B. Living with sexual limitations

If celibacy then, upon further reflection, may be retained as a sexual norm for the single adult, it is important to become as explicit as possible as to the problems, sexually speaking, that such a way of life may entail, and what might be done about them.

In attempting to do so, I must once again refer to the general considerations with which this section was begun (chapter 10) and also acknowledge, yet another time, the limited scope of what can be said here within the restrictions imposed both by the size of this particular book and my own experience. With these limitations in mind, three problems which confront many single persons in their attempts to cope with sexuality will be considered here: masturbation, fornication, and homosexuality.

1. Masturbation

Obviously a creative and joyful life as a celibate must rest squarely on the foundation of a frank confrontation with one's sexual potential and the realization of some kind of well-defined truce so far as its place in the experience of the celibate is concerned. This of course is far different from the "repression" of sex that people have so much come to fear since Freud. Repression is *un*conscious denial of sexual thoughts and feelings. That can only complicate our difficulties. By "confrontation" we refer to an open, conscious encounter with sexual feelings.

In this confrontation masturbation often asserts itself as the most viable alternative to complete denial of sexual experience. It was for this reason, as noted earlier, that it figured so large in the sexual sins of the medieval Catholic Church. For the celibate priests this was an ever-present sexual battlefront. As such, masturbation assumed an importance in the medieval Christian catalogue of sexual deviations out of all proportion to its dangers. It is this overseriousness that is now being rectified in modern sexual thinking. However, the balance of emphasis now has swung altogether too far in the other direction, as was argued in chapter six.

The issue to speak to here is how to terminate, or avoid in the first place, a masturbatory habit. Since so little has been written on this subject, and yet so many single people, I find, are troubled by it, I was gratified to come across a rather detailed analysis of just this issue in a book-length treatment of masturbation by David Cole. [1] Cole's discussion is all the more valuable in that he cannot be charged with harboring a negative attitude toward the practice and thereby branded "puritanical." If anything, he is too positive. But he does recognize that there can be legitimate reasons for terminating a masturbatory habit, and presents in some detail a therapeutic strategy for doing so. His approach is not unlike one that I have followed on several occasions in counseling, and in what follows I combine his suggestions with some of my own, again bearing in mind the general considerations discussed earlier.

It goes without saying, first of all, that to break with masturbation will require a deep desire to do so. Nothing can be accomplished where there is not the will for it.

The next step involves facing up to the magnitude of the sexual drive. It is important to recognize that far more is at stake in masturbation than a few moments of pleasure. One is coping here with the powerful urge to unite sexually with another. Since this cannot be realized satisfactorily outside of marriage, the celibate must forgo it altogether.

But how does one do that with so powerful an emotion? The answer lies in large part through interrupting the masturbatory or sexual thought process. By this more is meant than simply an unrefined use of willpower, whereby one simply repeats over and over again: I will not do it. Such broadside negativism is no more effective than incessant prayers of the same kind. They only serve to keep the thoughts preoccupied with the problem, whereas the objective should be to extinguish the thought process altogether.

In doing this two things should be kept clearly in focus: First, there *is* a human "I" over and above the human thought process. A person is not completely at one with his thinking. A person may stand over against the mental images flowing from his mind and is continuously selecting and rejecting what to center on. While awake a person repeatedly decides what to think about and what not to think about. "A man's words flow out of what fills his heart" (Lk. 6:45), Jesus said, apparently referring to the same reality.

A second thing to remember is that these images flowing from the mind are something like movie frames in the sense that they usually flash along in some kind of meaningful accumulative sequence. Looking now at the sexual thought process behind masturbation, it is apparent that it has a point of beginning in some tangible sexual stimuli or fantasy. To progress to masturbation, however, the fantasy must gain the consent of a person's attention. The fantasy is allowed to occupy the thought world. As the fantasy unfolds, it links up with sexual functions in the body. Psyche and soma, mind and body unite in a powerful drive forward toward sexual orgasm, and the further it progresses the more difficult it is to stop.

For anyone who wishes to break with masturbation then, the key issue is the interruption of the sexual thought process when the fantasy first asserts itself. This is not repression as it was defined earlier. This is the conscious decision to reject that particular mental process for another, a kind of decision that we constantly are making in our waking life.

This analysis also points up what is required in general if a celibate person is to live happily without sex. A firm decision must be made against all deviant sexual life, and this decision will have to take root in a deliberate effort to reject sexual fantasies at the point of their earliest intrusion into the thought life.

In addition of course positive things can be done. Loneliness and lethargy obviously present a vacuum in which the urge to unity which is at the heart of the sexual drive may rapidly increase its power over us. An active life with and for others can alleviate this to some extent, although, it should be said again, not necessarily provide a real substitute for that unique bond of unity which sexual intercourse creates. Sometimes it is suggested that sexual experience can be sublimated, that is transformed into other kinds of energy. There is no proof of this. But it cannot be doubted that sexual experience, powerful as it is, can definitely and creatively be *dis*placed by other meaningful activities, and this especially where there is the inner peace of a firm trust in God and readiness to live life in dialogue with His will.

2. Fornication

In a previous section of this study (chapter seven) on sexual disorders full discussion was given as to why fornication is harmful.

What however shall be done when sexual intercourse, apart from a marital commitment, has taken place? I am thinking here of those growing numbers of young people who, under the influence of modern attitudes toward premarital sex, have decided to experiment with sexual intercourse, discovering in the process that its consequences are indeed far different than they had thought. They are now asking themselves what responsibility they have for those with whom they related in this way, and what this will mean for their future sexual life in marriage.

Consider for example a young man troubled about sexual relations with a girl during his first year in college. At the time they were both out for a good time, in rebellion against church and home, and trying out new experiences. Their love for one another, he now clearly recognized some two years later, was very shallow, and neither of them entertained any real thought of marriage. And yet a shadow lingered. As he anticipated future relations to girls, and especially to the girl he would marry some day, a question persisted: Is he somehow obligated to that girl he had known so superficially, and yet had known sexually?

In one form or another I foresee this question coming up with increasing frequency in the years just ahead. The right answer, it must be strongly emphasized, must again be given contextually and only after thorough attention (within a counseling atmosphere) to all the relevant data. Our analysis of the sexual bond should make it clear that there are only differences of degree between what is called fornication and what is referred to as a unifying marital-sexual bond. Fornication is simply the perversion of a marital act through repression of its full significance.

Assuming that the persons involved do indeed want a responsible and loving solution in the aftermath of premarital sex, I would suggest the following:

1. Attend carefully to what extent the sexual bond formed was a meaningful one. If, for example, the love was real and freely given, and the bond formed is evident and strong, every

avenue should be explored to consolidate that relation as an ongoing marriage.

2. On the other hand if the relation was of that type, all too typical of contemporary sexual affairs, a passing act of experimentation, without the bond of love freely given and received, perhaps the best advice is to "forgive and forget."

3. Because, however, even superficial experimentation in sexual intercourse can leave its mark one should recommend a disclosure of such affairs to prospective husbands or wives. Sins of this kind are above all sins against the future marriage of the persons involved.

I trust that unmarried young people reading this section of the study who have never had sexual intercourse will find in the counsel given here a warning against complicating their lives or their future marriages by sexual adventures of this kind. The years of agonizing reappraisal that must often follow until these affairs can be decisively put to the past and new and more meaningful sexual bonds formed are surely a very high price to pay for a few moments of sexual pleasure.

3. Homosexuality

Single adults with homosexual tendencies face a very special set of challenges in living a celibate life. Anxiety about their masculinity or femininity may propel them into a vicious pattern of preoccupation with sexual matters. It is also apparent from the previous discussion of homosexuality that its origins may lie deep in the psychic (mental) events of early childhood and consequently its symptoms may impose themselves upon the persons involved as a fate scarcely to be borne.

For this reason the atmosphere of tolerance that enables persons to think and talk about this condition as seldom before in human history is certainly welcomed. In fact, here as elsewhere, honest confrontation with the problem at hand may be the first decisive step to resolve it. In any event one would certainly hope that persons who sense in themselves homosexual tendencies might find the strength to admit this and begin to talk about it to knowledgeable persons who could begin helping them sort out all that is involved.

That a sorting out process is possible, and that homosexual tendencies can be extinguished in favor of more normal sexual feelings, is now the growing conviction of a number of counseling psychologists and psychiatrists. [2] My own limited experience in counseling would confirm this new optimism, and would suggest the following as a minimum for those who would seek healing from this disorder [3]:

1. First of all, as Edmund Bergler also stresses in his book, *Homosexuality: Disease or Way of Life?* the persons involved must clearly and genuinely *want* to change. This may seem obvious, but failure to clarify this point may spell the difference between failure and success.

2. In addition, this "wanting" to change must issue in a firm decision to terminate all overt homosexual activities. This includes attention to those features in a given environment that are found to be activating of homosexual emotions. These should be avoided in a serious effort to curtail both homosexual fantasies and their physical fulfillment.

3. One must take care not to perpetuate the pattern of exclusive, preemptive "friendships," so characteristic of a homosexual lifestyle. These highly egocentric, tension-filled pairings can never really satisfy the social needs of those involved, and in shattering, almost always leave a trail of bad feelings in their wake. Here as elsewhere the emphasis should be instead on a growth process toward interpersonal freedom and mutuality.

4. Especially important for the homosexually inclined person who wants to change is a sustaining group where problems of self-understanding can be freely shared, ambivalent attitudes toward masculine and feminine roles acknowledged, and feedback over an extended period of time, both positive and negative, can be received and acted on.

In summary: The thesis with which this chapter began was that sexual healing for the unmarried, with celibacy as its goal, is by no means the impossibility it is sometimes made out to be in an age when life without sex is generally regarded as a tragedy of the highest order. Sexual life is indeed a great and wonderful good. But its absence should not be interpreted as the end of a worthwhile existence.

Perhaps all of us, married and unmarried alike, would be better off if we pondered some words of Jesus to the effect that in "heaven" there will be neither marriage nor giving in marriage. These words imply an experience beyond the boundaries of time and history when human sexuality will be transcended in some new and better form of living. That thought could serve as an antidote to the poison of Venus-worship which so infects these times.

summary and conclusion

The challenges that confront us as human beings so far as our sexuality is concerned are akin to the challenges that face us in many other aspects of our lives. Unlike the lower animals, we do not receive our life as a pattern of instincts. Rooted in nature, we are yet free to shape our lives to an unusual degree through the decisions that we make.

It is this "dignity" of freedom which allows us to ascend to the heights or sink to the depths.

Speaking more specifically to human sexuality, part of the difficulty seems to lie in not possessing a clear and unmistakable set of sexual instincts. Unlike sexual activity in the lower animals, we are not guided by "hormones," but exercise a unique sovereignty over sexual activity through our minds. And yet inborn sexual laws there obviously are. Whatever sovereignty we have in this area is not a freedom to do as we please. In the end we must encounter and live with our sexual nature as it really is. We can no more defy the laws of our sexual constitution and come out unhurt, then we can defy the laws of our gastronomical nature (digestive system) and not suffer the consequences. Sovereign we may be over what we eat, but we cannot decide what effect our choice of food will have on the health of our bodies. Sovereign we may be over how we behave sexually, but we are not free to decide what the results will be for our sexual well-being.

Free then as no other creatures on earth, human beings are challenged to exercise that freedom in favor of themselves and the way God made them. But how did God make us? What then are we sexually? What laws *are* written into the texture of our existence?

Until recently in the Western world, it was assumed that we knew the answers to these questions. The modern sexual revolution is fundamentally a crisis of doubt about those older answers, and a sometimes haphazard and often costly search for new ones.

As the basis for a Christian posture in the midst of the resulting sexual chaos, I have been urging:

(1) continuing respect for Jesus and His sharply formulated words of wisdom on sexual matters and especially (2) attention to His insight that human sexual experience creates a monogamous bond that no person should destroy.

In this light I have tried to survey the sexual trends of our time and exercise a constructive critique. The modern emphasis on "recreational sex" and "companionship marriage," I noted, may lead to dangerous repression of certain aspects of human sexuality. In the same way the new openness to masturbation, premarital and extramarital sex, and homosexuality as valid forms of sexual behavior could lead to the crippling of human sexuality, not to its fulfillment. Christian sexual healing summons us away from these destructive tendencies back to the pattern of sexual life given us by God. That those who hear this call will also experience unexpected grace in responding is at the heart of the gospel that Christianity is given to proclaim.

A particularly subtle and difficult challenge confronts those who would adopt such a point of view: the rapid transition from permanent to serial monogamy in Western society.

It was this "fiction" of divorce and remarriage as a cover-up for adultery that first elicited Jesus' words on human sexuality in His own time. His sayings to the effect that those who divorce and remarry are no less "committing adultery" than had they not gone to the trouble of legalizing their conduct are as disturbing today as when they were first spoken. Taken seriously they will require not only a *moral* confrontation between Christians and the world in which they now live, but an *institutional* conflict as well. Christians will not be able to accept the legal definitions of marriage designed by a North American society gone promiscuous any more than they could accept, in other settings, the institution of polygamy. Such confrontations are always difficult and weighted with the deepest emotions.

If, however, Jesus was right and the church remains loyal to His teachings it will see this emerging conflict as a service to the age, an essential feature of its mission to leaven and enlighten in His name a world always in struggle against darkness.

1. *Self-Love*, David Cole, 1969.
2. See for example Edmund Bergler, *Homosexuality, Disease or Way of Life?* Collier Books, 1962.
3. For a detailed and helpful discussion of treatment for men troubled by homosexuality, see *Changing Homosexuality in the Male* by Lawrence J. Hatterer. The observations and treatment methods recorded in this volume are the outgrowth of Dr. Hatterer's study of some 600 homosexual males over a period of 15 years.

appendix

1. Study Suggestions

In general I would recommend the practice of reading portions of the text together out loud in the study group. This can be done by letting each participant read a paragraph at a time, around the circle. This will provide a common basis for discussion, and the simple reading exercise itself will help some group members feel more relaxed and involved. If the group meets for less than one hour, the leader should choose only key paragraphs (those with italicized statements) in order to allow time for discussion.

Introduction

In discussing this introductory chapter, identify the kinds of attitudes and questions that the study group brings to a topic of this kind. Utilize the following "Sexual Attitudes Inventory" to do this. Have the study group members fill this out anonymously, then shuffle the papers (or books) and have them report and discuss the answers. Let them express freely their feelings without pressure to identify right or wrong solutions at this point.

Sexual Attitudes Inventory

Respond to the following statements, using this code: (a) strongly agree, (b) agree, (c) neutral, (d) disagree, (e) strongly disagree.

1. We should be able to discuss sexual matters frankly and openly in a discussion group of this kind (a b c d e).
2. The breakdown of sexual standards in society at large has begun to influence Christian thinking and conduct in the circles to which I belong (a b c d e).
3. My ideas on sex are clear on:
   — the place of sex in marriage (a b c d e).
   — the place of sex in the life of a single person (a b c d e).
   — what attitude to take toward premarital sexual relations (a b c d e).
   — what attitude to take toward extramarital sex (a b c d e).
   — what attitude to take toward divorce (a b c d e).
   — what attitude to take toward divorce and remarriage (a b c d e).
   — what attitude to take toward homosexuality (a b c d e).
   — what attitude to take toward masturbation (a b c d e).
   — what attitude to take toward pornographic literature (a b c d e).
4. The will of God for a Christian should be clear on matters of this kind (a b c d e).
5. Sexual standards should be taught by the Christian church and become requirements for membership in a Christian congregation (a b c d e).
6. Our sexual standards as Christians should be in harmony with the teachings of the Bible (a b c d e).
7. Our sexual standards should also be built on scientific knowledge about human sexuality (a b c d e).
8. The teachings of science are clear on sexual values (a b c d e).
9. In addition to setting standards the Christian church should take an active responsibility in sex education and not leave this entirely to the school or the home (a b c d e).
10. The church should also take an active role in helping people involved in sexual difficulties (a b c d e).

Chapter 1: Jesus' Teaching About Divorce and Remarriage

Note: Do not begin this first chapter without at least some discussion and insight into the material in the Introduction. This section is basic to understanding the basic assumptions of this book.

The study goal here is simply to understand this one short saying of Jesus. The study group may be surprised to learn that a single saying of Jesus would have circulated among the early Christians in different versions. They will not have thought about the fact that Jesus taught in Aramaic and that His teachings had to be translated into Greek (and then English!), nor that they were transmitted by word of mouth and used in the actual life of the church for a number of years before they were assembled and written down in the form that we have them in the Gospels.

If there is someone in your area (your minister?) who could explain this more fully, you might want to have him meet with you for this part of your study.

The saying itself is clear enough, even with the variations. By the end of the session each member of the class should have the ability to answer the following questions:

1. How many times does Jesus' teaching about divorce and remarriage appear in the New Testament? What are the most important variations in the saying?
2. Why does the saying in some instances speak only to men, in others to women as well?
3. In which versions of the saying do we find the "exception clauses"? What is the meaning of these "exception clauses"?
4. What is the form of this saying? What is the significance of its form?
5. What is the meaning of the saying, understood against the background of Jewish thought and practice in first-century Palestine? Ask each class member to write out his own paraphrase of the saying.

Chapter 2: Jesus' Teaching in Support of Monogamy

This is one of the most difficult and, at the same time, the most important of the chapters of this study. As in the previous chapter focus quite simply on understanding the "mind of

Christ." Check out especially the four main points on pages 18 to 20.

— Sexual life is good.
— The goal of human sexuality is monogamous marriage.
— The meaning of marriage is "one body."
— "What therefore God has joined together, let no man put asunder."

Be sure that each discussion group member understands these facets of Jesus' teaching, and especially the term "one body" or "one flesh" or as also referred to in this study, the marital-sexual bond. Discuss and compare the definitions of marriage which have been assumed by members of the study group.

Chapter 3: Jesus' Sexual Teaching and Sexual Thinking Today

The sex manual by David Reuben is quoted in this chapter. A group studying the issues touched on in this part of the inquiry might find it provocative to look more carefully at this widely circulated book or if some members have seen the Woody Allen movie spoof on the book, they might comment on it. As a graphic illustration of modern sexual thinking, passages from the opening section of chapter 4 (pp. 53 ff.) might be read. In this section Reuben introduces and further explains the classification system ("repro-sex," "love-sex," and "fun-sex") referred to in this chapter.

This chapter introduces some terms and concepts that may be difficult for some people. If the following terms will be difficult for some of your group members, define on a chalkboard: norms, biological science, physiology, neurology, psyche.

Chapter 4: Jesus' Marital Teachings and Marriage Today

After reading this chapter, find out which of the three models of marriage referred to are dominant in the thinking of those in the study group. Also, consider in greater detail Alvin Toffler's discussion of the future of marriage in the book referred to (*Future Shock*, Bantam edition, 1971). Additional paragraphs from his chapters on "The Odds Against Love" and "Temporary Marriage," pp. 249 ff., could serve as a focus for discussing where society is and where it is headed. Is Toffler's analysis correct? If so, what attitude should the Christian churches take to this emerging pattern of serial monogamy?

Chapter 5: Sexual Norms from Puberty to Marriage

There should be little difficulty in finding subject matter for vigorous group discussion in this chapter. One particularly urgent challenge facing the churches is sex education in the public schools. If the church would do more than criticize, it must ask itself how *it* would go about giving young people to-day the kind of sexual instruction they need. In fact, every Christian congregation should consider the possibility of puber-ty instruction classes, not to speak of education for those in older age brackets, within the context of the church itself. In these it could supplement the education being given in the public schools, with an emphasis on those particular values of special concern to Christians. This chapter affords the setting for a discussion of this possibility. In fact a study group might want to make the planning of such an instructional program one of the projects that might grow out of this entire study. Planning such a project could help the group members focus their own concerns in this area, as well as make a contribution to the life of the congregation or congregations of which they are members.

Discuss each of the four stages of sexual development out-lined in the chapter and comment on how Christian norms could be taught at each stage.

Chapter 6: Masturbation

Some study group members may find it difficult to discuss this topic openly. It might be well to raise this as a point of consideration before even beginning to do so. Young people experience ambivalent feelings about this practice, and the new emphasis in favor of masturbation has not changed this. If anything, it only increases the confusion. For this reason, a chance for an open discussion of masturbation could well be of great service to some in the study group, if not all.

Identify the two main reasons why masturbation is considered harmless and even beneficial. Identify the reasons why it might be abnormal and harmful, especially if retained as a sexual way of life.

Chapter 7: Fornication

For many this is one of the most urgent of contemporary sexual questions: what attitude to take toward premarital sex? A significant increase in fornication, particularly among women, is taking place in modern society. If Christians are to counteract this trend, they will need to know what the dangers are, and begin teaching their youth in a straightforward, intelligent, and realistic way about them. Again, the material provided should offer stimulus for discussion, providing there is the freedom to do so.

Again examine and evaluate the basic reasons why premarital sex is considered normative, even beneficial to many, and what might be said in opposition to this pattern and thought.

Many short films and filmstrips are available on premarital sex and sexual relationships. From a local library; Audiovisuals, Box 370, Elkhart, Ind. 46514; or Audio Visual Library, Box 347, Newton, Kan. 67114; order one of these films and compare the approach to that presented in this chapter. Films for other sessions are also available and could be used with good results.

Chapter 8: Adultery

As a challenge to churches adultery may not seem at the moment to be such an immediate threat. The strictures against it have been strong and clear. But if that is the case, it may only be the calm before the storm, for the attack on the negative attitude of the Christian and Jewish traditions against adultery is now in full swing. No one should feel it wasted time to consider in depth why adultery is wrong. The problem is more complicated than is usually recognized as the material in this chapter will indicate. Put to work here the insights and note the definitions of marriage discussed in this and previous chapters.

Chapter 9: Homosexuality

For additional information about homosexuality of the kind that might be needed in a discussion of this topic, the Reuben paperback, *Everything You Always Wanted to Know About Sex*, might be useful. This may also be the time to invite a professional counselor, if such a person is available, to contribute to the study. This person could speak to the group, not only about homosexuality, but about some of the other topics dealt with both in this and the following section of this study.

110

Chapter 10: Sexual Healing, General Considerations

The six general therapeutic guidelines described in this chapter might well be the focus for the discussion here. Are they understood? Does the study group agree with them? Point 5 should be given special consideration by a study group associated with a congregation. Does the congregation involved provide somewhere in its life a therapeutic setting for people with sexual problems, not to speak of other difficulties? Should it?

Chapter 11: Sexual Healing for the Married

This is no doubt the most difficult section of the whole study. Specific help in the face of specific sexual problems demands a high degree of tact, wisdom, and insight. Apart from the materials offered for discussion in this chapter, the leader might want to center the class discussion on some specific instances of marital difficulty, fictional or otherwise, as a way of further clarifying the approach to marital problems being suggested here. This chapter is not intended to replace the role of a psychiatrist to give formal sessions for some form of overt sexual disorder, rather it is a basic framework from which to develop insight.

Chapter 12: Sexual Healing for the Unmarried

Do those in the study group accept the idea of celibacy (sexual abstinence) for single people? Look at each of the four points made under the section, "Celibacy as a Valid Way of Life." Did the single adults in your congregation ever have a retreat together to consider the problems and opportunities unique to their situation? Would they want more discussion along this line? Invite your pastor to share the approach he takes to the problems mentioned in the section, "Living with Sexual Limitations."

Summary and Conclusion

Review the territory covered. It might be interesting to repeat the "Sexual Attitudes Inventory" used in the introductory part of this study. Has there been any progress? Try to identify what learning has taken place and what questions still remain.

2. Bibliographical Suggestions

(See also the footnotes at the conclusion of each chapter in the preceding study.)

a. The volume, *Sexuality and Man*, compiled and edited by the Sex Information and Education Council of the United States, Charles Scribner's Sons, 1970, has an excellent annotated bibliography, as well as extensive listings (with comments) of available film resources for sex education programs. It also provides concise summaries of the prevailing modern points of view on most of the relevant sexual topics.

b. Otto Piper's volume, *The Christian Interpretation of Sex*, Scribner's, 1955, is an especially fine study of human sexuality from the biblical perspective. Also Richard Hettlinger's *Living with Sex: the Student's Dilemma*, Seabury, 1966, merits special mention for its intelligent and Christian handling of sexual issues as they confront the college age young person.

c. Several cross-disciplinary studies, written by Christian psychiatrists or anthropologists, have proven helpful. One of these, written in a simple, vivid style that makes it attractive for use with young adults, is the book by the Canadian Psychiatrist, M. O. Vincent, *God, Sex and You*, Lippincott, 1971. The religious historian, E. O. James, in his book *Marriage Customs Through the Ages*, Collier Books, 1965, provides a unique integration of anthropological and Christian perspectives.